The Confident Writing Teacher

Cultivating Meaningful Writing in Middle School

SHELLEY BARKER

HEINEMANN
Portsmouth, NH

Heinemann

361 Hanover Street

Portsmouth, NH 03801–3912

www.heinemann.com

Offices and agents throughout the world

The author and publisher wish to thank those who have generously given permission to reprint borrowed material:

Excerpt from the Common Core State Standards © Copyright 2010. National Governors Association Center for Best Practices and Council of Chief State School Officers. All rights reserved.

Library of Congress Cataloging-in-Publication Data

Barker, Shelley.

The confident writing teacher : cultivating meaningful writing in middle school / Shelley Barker.

pages cm

Includes bibliographical references.

ISBN 978-0-325-02168-3

1. English language—Composition and exercises—Study and teaching (Middle school).

2. Language arts (Middle school). I. Title.

LB1631.B258 2013

428.00712—dc23

2013016447

Editor: Tobey Antao

Production editor: Sonja S. Chapman

Typesetter and interior design: Shawn Girsberger

Cover design: Suzanne Heiser

Author photo: Jennifer Locke

Manufacturing: Steve Bernier

Printed in the United States of America on acid-free paper

17   16   15   14   13   EBM   1   2   3   4   5

FOR GREG

*I'll be forever thankful my summer camp
went co-ed so we could find each other.*

Contents

Acknowledgments

I'VE ALWAYS BELIEVED IT'S THE PEOPLE ON THE JOURNEY that make our lives worth living. Thanks and undying gratitude go out to:

Past and present students, staff, and parents from Centennial Middle School in Snohomish, Washington. I always tell people I work at the most amazing school, and it's true. Thank you for filling my days with laughter, discovery, and purpose. I want to be a better person and a better teacher because of all of you! Proud to be a Patriot, always.

My friend and colleague, Carolyn Coombs, who stood by me from day one and encouraged me along the way. I miss teaching down the hall from you, but I know you do your good works where you are needed.

My teaching partner and partner in crime, Kathy Williams. Our shared brain and loud laughing tendencies make my every day! Thank you for always finding the funny, for appreciating middle schoolers for who they are, and for sitting by me in those meetings where all we hear are crickets. I could not do this job without you!

Fellow teacher and writer Megan Sloan, who started the ball rolling by saying, "I'm going to give my editor a call . . . ." Thanks for your support, your advice, and our Starbucks meet-ups. Your calm perspective is always appreciated.

My parents, Jay and Estelle King. You put my feet on this path! How will I ever thank you for that? Love you both.

Patty Adams, Lisa Fowler, Kim Cahill, Suzanne Heiser, Sarah Fournier, and the entire production team at Heinemann. Thank you for making my first journey into the publishing world smooth and as stress-free as possible. You are all the best!

My editor, Tobey Antao, who took on a project started by someone else and stuck with me to the very end. Thank you for your patience, your wise perspectives, your encouragement, and our phone conversations that always seemed to end up in fits of laughter. You are truly the best!

My children, Matt, Kate, and Jake, who put up with a whole lot of "Shhh, Mom's writing." I could not ask for kinder, funnier, more appropriately irreverent children! You all are my pride and joy. Love you to the moon and back!

And finally, my husband, Greg, who took up the slack, listened to me whine, stopped me from pitching my laptop out the window, cooked meals, and said annoying things like, "Don't you have a book to write?" when apparently I was procrastinating. I can't imagine this life with anybody but you! xxoo

Introduction

PICTURE A CLASSROOM OF MIDDLE SCHOOLERS in their goofy and clumsy glory, like Labrador retriever puppies, all limbs, all movement, all noise. They are starving to death fifteen minutes after they've eaten lunch. They fall out of their chairs for no apparent reason. Their battle cry is, "That's not fair!" and they use it with great skill and finesse. They get themselves into the strangest situations imaginable. Their preferences change like the wind. They are the picture of unpredictability and silliness.

Got it? Now add this.

You announce the next class writing project. Four kids smile quietly to themselves because they love to write. Several roll their eyes, one so skillfully you're pretty sure she got a good glimpse of her brain. A few more just stare at you because, well, they're cool. The majority of the students launch into dramatic renditions of the torture you've just introduced into their lives. They fling their bodies across desks and chairs. The backs of their hands drape across their foreheads. They utter an agonizing, "Nooooo! Not writing! Anything but writing!" Three kids put their heads on their desks with a gentle thunk, wishing writing would simply disappear.

■ The Reality

We've all been there. As teachers, we know that the ability to communicate through writing is an important skill our students will need and use their entire lives. Through high school, college, on the job, in the community, they'll need to write to inform, to support causes, to change minds, to change the world! Some may, if they get over their aversion, discover that they like to write and make it their profession. We might have future poets in our midst or people who will write poems as birthday gifts to their loved ones. We get the awesome power behind writing, but the kids who sit before us don't see it and don't love it.

Our students were once little kids who loved to tell stories. What happened to them? When young, they dictated their tales to an adult. As their writing skills developed, they joyfully wrote and illustrated their own work. Maybe they found that as they got older, writing got confusing. As the rules increased, so did their insecurities. Maybe they became frustrated when papers they'd put their hearts and souls into came back covered in red ink (it doesn't take long to dislike something that always makes you feel like a failure). Maybe you experienced these feelings yourself as a student.

Many kids in our schools today are frustrated with writing. They know they are supposed to produce text, but they aren't always sure how to go about it. Sometimes the assigned prompts are about something they're not interested in; they don't know what to write if they don't have anything to say. The result, sadly, is that many kids say they don't like to write. Many write to fulfill an assignment, not to create something meaningful. Some refuse to write at all.

■ What's Possible

What if your middle school writing classroom looked like this:

» Kids write and write and write—real writing—and legitimately use the writing process, maybe for the first time in their lives.

» Students show you they are becoming writers by the questions they ask, the ways they use the writing process, their approach to solving writing problems, and the writing conversations they initiate.

» Lessons serve a purpose, and students see clearly how new skills fit beautifully with their writing progress.

» Students are connected to you and to one another.

» There is a culture of collaboration, honesty, and (dare we say it) fun.

» Students are confident in their abilities to tackle any writing task, from memoirs to standardized tests. Writing may not be their favorite thing to do, but they know how to do it and they do it well.

» Kids feel safe to take risks and show their true selves. They laugh easily and cry if they need to.

» Thirty-two kids are working on thirty-two different projects at thirty-two levels of writing ability—something others might see as chaos waiting to happen—and you're delighted: it's your goal.

» You need the kids and the kids need you. You don't want to disappoint one another.

Something incredible happens when we hand over the responsibility of writing to our students and then act as their guide. We approach writing instruction differently: the kids make the writing their own (which it should be in the first place) and we give them the instruction and evaluation they need. Suddenly writing means something. Kids are attached to what they produce. ("Hey, when are we getting our poems back? I'm suffering some separation anxiety.") Their writing becomes a part of them.

▮ What's Ahead

This book is a practical guide that will help you help your students produce all kinds of meaningful text. After taking a moment to reflect on the writing experiences in your own life, you'll find out how to prepare an environment designed for middle school writers. You'll be introduced to writing lessons and experiences your students need to make incredible improvements in their composition skills. You'll also find out how to evaluate your students' writing in ways that move them forward and make writing a process of always getting better, not just getting a good grade.

As you apply what you've learned, you and your students will begin to notice changes, both in their abilities and in their attitudes toward writing. Don't be surprised when the kids who daily told you how much they loathed writing say they want to be authors when they grow up! You may find yourself torn between yelling "I told you so!" and breaking into a happy dance. I suggest avoiding both; watching teachers shouting and dancing tends to freak middle school kids out. (Of course, if that's your intention. . . .)

What About the Common Core State Standards?

You may be saying, "Well, that sounds great, but we live in a time of standards! My students have to pass a standardized test!" You're right. The Common Core State Standards now guide instruction in the majority of states in the nation.

Whenever standards are issued, we run the great risk of turning their requirements into our curriculum rather than using them to guide our instruction. Teaching to the test is a narrow experience for students, especially in a subject as deep and rich as writing. But it's no surprise that standards often become the sole foundation of instruction, especially when school ratings and teacher evaluations depend on whether the standards are met or not.

Rest assured that the instructional ideas you'll encounter here will allow your students to demonstrate their writing skills on standardized tests. However, instead of simply creating test takers, you'll produce skilled and confident writers, prepared to face *any* writing situation. The authors of the Common Core State Standards (www.corestandards.org) make this very clear:

> Standards are not curriculum. This initiative is about developing a set of standards that are common across states. The curriculum that follows will continue to be a local responsibility (or state-led, where appropriate). The curriculum could become more consistent from state to state based on the commonality of the standards; however, there are multiple ways to teach these standards, and therefore, there will be multiple approaches that could help students accomplish the goals set out in the standards.

Through what you encounter in the following chapters, you'll be able to prepare your students for their writing futures—academic, test-related, or creative.

▌Here We Go!

It is well within your power to produce skilled and confident writers. Let the ideas in this book help shape your instructional beliefs as you design a writing program for your classes. You may find yourself teaching writing in a way you never considered and getting results you never dreamed possible. Ready? Let's get started!

1

The Evolving Cycle of Teaching Writing

THE DIAGRAM IN FIGURE 1.1 shows the cycle you might travel in becoming a confident and competent teacher of writing. Step 1 begins in the center; steps 2 through 6 continue around the circle, spiraling upward thereafter, with each step revisited in light of the growing complexity generated by experience and increased skill.

2
Strengthen your confidence
Plan an environment for young writers

3
Build confidence each day
Become the teacher you wish you'd had

6
Celebrate increased student confidence and skill

1
Jump-start your confidence
What's your writing history?

4
Cultivate writing practices
Increase writing confidence by giving students what they need

5
Respond authentically
Build writing skill and confidence through thoughtful evaluation of students' writing

Figure 1.1

Step 1. Jump-Start Your Confidence: What's Your Writing History?

The center of the diagram represents a teacher's level of confidence as a writer, as well as her feelings about her abilities as a writing teacher. *How* writing manifests itself in a middle school classroom begins with the teacher. A confident writing teacher is at ease with the nature of writing. She realizes that writing is a process that is messy and difficult yet rewarding and fruitful. She does not walk into a classroom knowing all the answers. She is at ease with questions and realizes that by saying, "I've struggled with writing clear dialogue too; let's work together and see what we can figure out," she becomes her students' authoritative and reassuring writing partner.

> *How* writing manifests itself in a middle school classroom begins with the teacher.

She knows what her students need because she writes herself. She has lived the struggle inherent in writing, coming out on the other side as a more polished and skillful writer. She has experienced firsthand the natural frustration writing brings. She understands that writing the contents of one's heart and mind is made to look easy by those who do it well.

She welcomes all learners into her classroom, knowing that not everyone will begin at the same place, and that's okay—it's the nature of becoming a better writer. The underlying expectation in her classroom is that everyone, no matter her or his experiences or abilities, moves forward and makes progress as a writer each day.

Step 2. Strengthen Your Confidence: Plan an Environment for Young Writers

The benefits of this stage are twofold: as a writing teacher identifies and sets up the conditions that allow middle school students to thrive in the writing workshop, he starts to feel a sense of accomplishment in embarking on this new way of thinking about writing instruction. During this stage he envisions his classroom environment and what will and will not happen there. Through this upfront thinking and planning, his desires and expectations for his classroom become more refined, and the fear of the unknown often present in a new situation diminishes.

As a confident middle school writing teacher he knows that students need an environment designed for writers and writing. He understands that different stages of the writing process—from oral activities like minilessons and writing groups to silent moments when writers go inside their heads to create text that reflects their unique view of the world—require different conditions. He acknowledges that students who feel safe with their fellow student writers and with him are honest in their writing. Students who feel safe do not fear for their dignity as thinkers and writers.

> **Students who feel safe do not fear for their dignity as thinkers and writers.**

Step 3. Build Confidence Each Day: Become the Teacher You Wish You'd Had

Here a writing teacher considers her own transformation as a middle school writing teacher and how those changes will impact her classroom. Thinking like a writer, she envisions what students will need to function in writerly ways. She considers the physical, cognitive, and emotional development of her students and thinks carefully about the kinds of writing lessons that will meet these needs. She begins to create systems that help young writers keep track of their thoughts, notes, and drafts. She thinks about what she needs as a writer and how she'll create those same situations for her students.

> **...while some writing is meant to be kept personal, the power of written words multiplies when shared.**

She believes that while some writing is meant to be kept personal, the power of written words multiplies when shared. She knows that a group of middle school peers, with a structure to guide them, can provide helpful and necessary feedback to one another. She introduces writing groups and models how a writing group functions. She knows the power of publishing, of sharing one's words with a larger group when the time is right. She arranges opportunities for paper-and-ink publishing, online publishing, open-mic sessions, and other chances for students to share their writing throughout the school and community. Sharing like this creates and strengthens the school's writing culture. Writing becomes "something we do around here."

She knows her behavior impacts students' willingness to develop authentic writing. She views herself as different from the average teacher. She doesn't see her job as imparting knowledge but rather as guiding students on the tricky journey that begins with a blank page and ends with a beautifully crafted memoir, poem, story, essay, or letter. This guidance approach changes how she and her students interact; she leaves me-teacher-you-student instruction at the door. Students see her as a more knowledgeable writing partner. She models her own writing processes and struggles. She shares her best and worst work so students gain an accurate and realistic perception of what writing is.

However, she doesn't view the comfortable give-and-take of the writing process as being loose and without purpose. She understands that middle school writers need structure, boundaries, and, once in a while, a firm nudge in the right direction. She knows that while her classroom may not look or feel like other classrooms, chaos has no place there. She understands that part of the sense of safety surrounding her student writers is the confidence they have that she is in charge, that she will not tolerate inappropriate behavior; she has high expectations for how her students treat one another and holds them to these expectations.

Step 4. Cultivate Writing Practices: Increase Writing Confidence by Giving Students What They Need

Now a writing teacher considers what kinds of instruction and writing practices will benefit the middle school students in his writing workshop. A confident middle school writing teacher recognizes the conditions required for lessons that endure, as well as special considerations for middle school learners. He knows that if students are to develop their writing skills and confidence, they need to push outside their comfort zones, move beyond the solitary act of drafting, and share what they've written with others. He knows this talk is important and necessary. He understands that writing conversations can be formal and informal. He believes that when writers talk about their writing and the writing of others, they clarify and solve problems, come up with ideas, and encourage one another. He also understands that, though scary, standing before others to read one's work is an important part in students' writing development. As frightening as this public display can be, writers who step out of the familiar and comfortable come away even more enriched in their writing skills and confidence.

> ...if students are to develop their writing skills and confidence, they need to push outside their comfort zones, move beyond the solitary act of drafting, and share what they've written with others.

Step 5. Respond Authentically: Build Writing Skill and Confidence Through Thoughtful Evaluation of Students' Writing

In any learning situation, we all need feedback to grow and become more skilled. Evaluating writing has its own set of unique challenges, including how to best respond and how to consider a grade for something as subjective as written composition. A writing teacher knows that if she is to develop skilled and competent writers, her feedback must do more than focus on that which is easy to identify as right or wrong—that is, conventions. Balanced evaluations let students know what they've done well and what they need to do to make improvements. She builds her students' confidence but not in ways that lead students to doubt her sincerity. She offers feedback that is specific and thoughtful. She also knows that students must learn to gauge their own writing success, not depend on the observations of others. By gradually releasing

> ...students must learn to gauge their own writing success, not depend on the observations of others.

responsibility, she develops independent writers who trust their own evaluations.

Step 6. Celebrate Increased Student Confidence and Skill

At this point middle school writers begin to produce writing that is authentic and purposeful. A writing teacher has created a place that offers a writing experience like no other. Instead of balking at the added independence and responsibility, students write because they know that what they have to say matters. Writing changes from a task the teacher makes kids do to a way for them to think about and process their own thinking. Students view themselves as writers, not as someone forced to write. They see the necessity for a writing process. Again and again they've heard their teachers stress the importance of prewriting, drafting, revising, editing, and producing a final draft. Now, possibly for the first time, the usefulness of the writing process becomes real. They understand that writing is not just setting down a series of events: "First we went to the park. Then we played tag on the monkey bars. I fell and split my forehead. Then the ambulance came. I got six stitches." The writing process becomes a tool with purpose, and there is a reason to revise. The phrase "clarity in writing" has new meaning. Students understand an audience will read what they produce; making sure thoughts and feelings are accurately portrayed takes on a new urgency.

> A confident writing teacher creates an encouraging environment.... Composition remains a personal act but becomes less egocentric.

During this time, a confident writing teacher creates an encouraging environment by providing choice, support, possibilities, and relevant instruction. Her students take amazing strides forward. Gone are the outlandish stories about aliens landing on earth and attacking innocent people who are saved by some burly seventh graders (mainly, the author and his six best friends). Composition remains a personal act but becomes less egocentric. The notion of audience takes hold. Students learn that words composed in a meaningful way have power and can affect the outlooks and opinions of others.

The changes in the writing teacher's own attitudes toward and practices in writing instruction impact her students. They abandon the thought that they cannot write and replace it with the idea that, at the very least, they know where to start developing an idea. She notices students beginning to edit and revise on their own (a benchmark she can count on as young writers develop). She hears students profess a desire for clarity ("so my reader can really understand my message," as Annie, one of my seventh graders, pointed out). Writing starts to take place outside the classroom, in journals, on computers, and on the backs of take-out food bags. Students enter class on Monday morning eager to add something that happened over the weekend to their list of writing topics. Middle school writers, armed with pens and paper, confidence and a cause, light up the world with their energy. At this point, a middle school writing teacher realizes the wisdom in simply stepping aside, becoming an unobtrusive guide, and letting her students write.

All the thinking, planning, doing, and evaluating come together in students who are skilled and confident writers. Under her guidance, students begin learning *how* to be writers rather than *what* to write. Kids take charge of their composition. Because they have come from an environment of encouragement, they are comfortable not always knowing the answers, confident they have the skills to find their way. They know they have the skills to communicate no matter the subject. Writing has become part of them, another way to communicate the contents of their minds. They are less likely to become one of those adults paralyzed by fear when asked to write something.

It's Worth It in the End: New and Improved Teacher Confidence

The completed cycle feeds a writing teacher's confidence as a writer and a writing instructor. His students' success renews his desires to develop his classroom's writing atmosphere, create and present appropriate and meaningful minilessons, and encourage his students as they struggle and succeed. He gets positive feedback from his students, their parents, and himself as he reflects on his instruction.

Just as there is no prescribed amount of time in which to accomplish each step, there is no set number of times a teacher can make his way through the cycle. And like the writing process, the cycle may get messy, and the steps may take place in a different order from the one presented here. That is fine. The important thing to remember is that the cycle nurtures everyone in the middle school writing classroom, including the teacher.

Cynical readers may dismiss these scenarios and ideas as looking better than they work. We've all felt that way after reading a book on educational theory or practice or attending a professional workshop or conference. However, please know that what I share with you in this book is what I believe to be true. I write about the possibilities for classrooms centered on writing because a middle school writing classroom is where I live and breathe. If you wonder whether this approach to writing instruction can work as described, stay with me. We'll dig in to each step in the cycle, experiencing the joys as well as the bumps in the road. I'll share with you practical processes and activities that will help you get your writing outlook, your writing instruction, and your writing students pointed in the right direction.

The longer I teach, the more I believe that teaching and learning are all about the relationships we form and the connections we make. I'm suggesting that kids in middle school tell us they hate to write because they've not had the chance to truly connect with written words. If we want our schools to turn out young adults who know and use writing as a viable method of self-expression, who are as comfortable picking up a pen as they are picking up a phone, we have to capitalize on this precious time called adolescence. We need to see this sometimes tough transition from childhood to adulthood as a chance to develop something amazing: the knowledge that words can change the world.

> ... kids in middle school tell us they hate to write because they've not had the chance to truly connect with written words.

I'm pretty sure the students in my classes each fall would *not* call writing a gift from me to them. The majority of them either profess dislike or indifference toward written expression. I know this because every year, the same scenario develops: It's seventh-grade orientation night. Sixth graders, looking worried and apprehensive, raise tentative hands, asking questions about lockers, changing classes, whether middle school teachers really throw away papers without a name on them. I tell them it won't take long to understand lockers and hallways, and that middle school teachers are kind people who try to identify who submitted a paper before tossing it.

Then my teaching partner tells them that language arts at our school is a writing class. The room gets quiet. A (very) few of our future students whisper "Yes!" under their breaths, but the majority have a look of horror on their faces. A few brave ones, already a mile or two down the road of adolescence, roll their eyes toward the ceiling, an oh-great look on their face. My partner and I look at each other and grin.

If they only knew that earlier that very day I'd told my current seventh graders, the ones sitting before me at this same orientation a year ago, that their culminating project for language arts is to write twenty-six pages, one for each letter of the alphabet, about themselves. Those pages must showcase everything they've learned about writing in the previous eight months. Each year I wait for their reactions. Each year I'm rewarded with confident faces showing no visceral reaction to such a sizeable writing project. Instead I hear things like "Cool!" and "I've been waiting all year for this!" and "I remember when my sister did this project; she took her book with her to college last fall!"

I can say in full confidence that writing doesn't have to be something students loathe. We can be agents of change in helping create a generation of people who do not, as many adults today tell me they do, hate to write because they think they cannot write. If the pen truly is mightier than the sword, imagine the impact we can make!

2

Jump-Starting Your Confidence

What's Your *Writing Story?*

WHEN I WAS IN FOURTH GRADE, my teacher was scheduled to retire halfway through the school year. Looking back, I wonder if she decided that the last five months of her decades-long career were going to be full of the things she liked best about teaching: art, music, and reading. These were, of course, the days before standardized testing and accountability, so it wasn't unusual for a teacher to go her own way. I don't remember doing a lot of math that year. Social studies? Science? Geography? Nonexistent. We sang constantly, and I learned to play the Flute-o-Phone. We put on plays and baked cookies and listened as she read *The Secret Garden* and *Little Lord Fauntleroy* to us.

My fourth-grade teacher also set out to make our writing better, or so she told us. In one of our many art classes, we constructed snowmen out of paper, and we proudly posted our creations on the back wall of the classroom. These snowmen were meant to serve a dual purpose: they would not only create a festive scene before the holidays but also help us become better writers. After our snowmen were posted, we were told to go to the back of the room and tear a bit of them away every time we made an error in our writing. Our snowmen diminished in direct proportion to our incorrect spelling, missing punctuation, and sloppy grammar.

I worked hard to keep my snowman whole. Sadly, the day I had to take the walk of shame and tear away a piece of my creation is one of my most vivid memories of that year. I'd misspelled the word *cabin* in my story about a girl who went to summer camp. With its soft *a* sound, I reasoned there must be two consonants following the vowel: *cabbin*. My teacher pointed out the error of my ways, and my snowman was no longer complete. Almost forty years later, guess what I think about each and every time I write the word *cabin*?

My grown-up self wishes my spelling error had played out differently. I wish my teacher had stopped by my desk and simply said, "Hey, *cabin* has one *b* instead of two." Word nerd that I am, I would not have forgotten it. Better yet, I wish my teacher had stopped by my desk and asked me to read my story to her. I wish she'd listened carefully and maybe commented on how my description of the cabin made her feel like she was right there and how my line "ten tall trees" was an example of something called *alliteration* and that sometimes writers use alliteration to put a little fun into their writing.

As an adult and a teacher, I've found that many of us have painful memories of learning to write. Over the years, I've had the great pleasure of teaching seminars on writing instruction. Classes often become confessionals in which perfectly intelligent, capable, and talented adults admit that the writing experiences they had as children still affect them today. Mostly, I've found out that I am not alone, that plenty of us have snowman stories and that the emotions associated with these defining moments are still raw. One woman told me that when it came time to write something, *anything*, she felt paralyzed and physically ill. Couple that with being an English teacher who is expected to teach her students to write, and you have one stressed-out instructor!

If you are currently a member of the teaching profession, it is very likely that you were never taught to write. Shocked? Think about it. Certainly, we wrote, but what did writing *instruction* look like when you were a kid? Do you remember receiving any? I was a child of the seventies, and I do not remember being taught to write. My teachers assumed that if I knew how to read and knew the function of each word in a sentence, I was able to compose. This assumption is true about very few children, then and now. My language arts teachers focused on those things that could be measured

> **If you are currently a member of the teaching profession, it is very likely that you were never taught to write.**

and counted as right or wrong, like parsing sentences, identifying linking verbs, and making sure those darned participles didn't dangle. No one taught me to write engaging leads, and certainly no one told me that the writing I did should be a reflection of my thinking. Worksheets on which we filled in all the missing commas were much easier and faster to grade.

Take a walk down memory lane, and remember writing when you were a kid. What feelings are stirred up when you think about the writing you did in school? Do you have a specific memory around writing? What is it? How does that specific memory impact your feelings about your writing today? How does it impact how you approach writing in your classroom?

English Teachers Who Think They Can't Write

Frankly, my biggest worry is that my students will be better writers than I am, and then what? I'm supposed to be their English teacher, the one who knows writing inside and out, but if I share my work with them, it's possible they'll find out I can't write. That scares me more than anything.

—Fourth-grade language arts teacher (name withheld)

If you, too, find yourself in this situation, you are not alone. Most of us who teach English didn't go into it for the love of writing; we majored in English because we loved literature. It is love of story, not composition, that compels us to teach language arts. Most of us know enough about writing to move along, assigning prompts and research papers, but it's literature that sustains us. To compensate, we make sure our writing assignments are planned to the last possible variable—we cover all the bases, leaving students little room to fail. Unfortunately, at the same time, we box our students in.

In high school my daughter was given an assignment to write a poem that reflected on the image of the mockingbird in *To Kill a Mockingbird*. Everything she was to include was relegated, right down to the rhyme scheme, the number of metaphors, and the line count. I can tell you what this assignment killed: my daughter's desire to express herself through poetry. She was much more concerned about following the rules than writing a poem that created strong images and meaning through a beautiful collection of words. While there is nothing wrong with structure, we must beware of stressing format over thought. Are we structuring to allow students to be skillful, creative, and independent writers or to be able to remain in our own comfort zones?

After examining your past writing instruction, you may start chastising yourself for having permanently damaged your former students. (On sleepless nights I often contemplate the staggering number of students to whom I should apologize for what I've done to their writing confidence.) But stick with me here: do the hard work, and I promise you'll come through this with a better understanding of your writing past, how it affects your present reality, and your future as a writing teacher.

The kids in our classrooms are in many ways no different from us when we were kids. Some students come to us with the "gift." These students will flourish as writers in spite of us. For whatever reason, they get how words go to together to form stories, poems, and essays. As I encounter these talented writers, I cannot explain their ability any more than I can explain the ability of a gifted athlete or a gifted musician: the potential is simply there, and the writing comes easily.

Think about the natural writers you've encountered in your classroom in the past. What percentage of your students arrives with this gift? My guess is one or two percent. The rest fall somewhere in between "I almost get it" and "this writing stuff makes *no* sense to me."

Right now, this moment, you have the chance to accomplish two things at once. As you begin coming to terms with your own writing history, you'll also start to prepare a new road for all your students, from the skilled writers to the nonwriters. Use those feelings you had as a kid, the confusion about the words circled in red, the comments you couldn't understand, the times you worked outside the box only to be reprimanded for not following the format or the teacher's instructions. Remember how your young feelings were hurt by the sometimes careless statements your teachers made about something as heartfelt and personal as writing. Take your experiences, and turn them into the positive and productive opportunities you'll provide for your students. Teachers are called to make the world a better place, one child at a time. You can be the teacher who makes writing work for kids.

> "Take what you need; leave the rest." Please apply this idea to your own writing past. Take what you need—the positive experiences, the times when you felt successful, the times when writing made sense to you—and leave the rest—the red ink, the negative or empty comments, the references to your spelling and penmanship.

One of my undergraduate professors had a great catchphrase I'll borrow here. Whenever she presented us with new ideas or material, she'd say, "Take what you need; leave the rest." Please apply this idea to your own writing past. Take what you need—the positive experiences, the times when you felt successful, the times when writing made sense to you—and leave the rest—the red ink, the negative or empty comments, the references to your spelling and penmanship. (But do keep a small dose of those powerful feelings tucked away to remind yourself that you never want your students to experience what you did.) From here on, you get to create a new situation for yourself, one in which you may begin to look at your own writing in a totally different way.

■ Taking the First Step

My favorite Pacific Northwest lifestyle magazine recently ran an article on guerilla gardening. In addition to the interesting concept, I was captivated by the idea of just letting a garden happen. The author advises people to let go of the stress of gardening and just stick plants in the ground. If it works, great; if not, move on.

My palms started to sweat. Just stick plants in the ground? Are you kidding me? A litany of what-ifs raced through my brain. What if the conditions aren't right? What if the plant grows best in the shade, and I put it in direct sunlight? What if the dreadful clay soil our house sits on does not provide the proper nutrients? How could this successful gardener, who has written books and has a website, say such careless things?

My uncertainty stems both from inexperience and from bad experiences. I haven't spent enough time gardening to know what works and what doesn't. I haven't read enough books, talked to enough people, and tried enough plant combinations to know any better. And when I did finally take the plunge and dropped a few hundred dollars at the local nursery, the plants failed to thrive, making me throw my hands in the air and say, "See? Dead! I am *not* a gardener."

We all come to our beliefs through our experiences. As a gardener who has experienced a fair amount of failure, there are things I could do to make my garden grow. I could take classes and talk with the cranky lady who works at the nursery's information desk. I could read books and examine what I see happening in my garden. I could think about plants and dirt and compost and earthworms. While any and all of the above activities could be beneficial, they won't be *until I actually do them.*

Here's where *you* do, where you take the first brave step. It involves a pen, some paper, and you, but before you get nervous about being asked to write, consider these self-imposed ground rules:

1. The writing you do is yours and yours alone. No one gets to read what you've written unless you extend an invitation to do so.

2. The writing you do doesn't have to amount to anything. Your conventions and penmanship do not have to be perfect. Something you write may begin to take shape and develop into a great future writing topic, but don't go into this exercise with that expectation. Just write and let it happen.

3. Use this exercise to face the past. Stand up to it, and be honest. If you have a story like my snowman story, recognize it for the unfortunate situation it was. Give it form on paper and then let it go, realizing that through that experience you are going to become the teacher that all kids deserve.

4. Set a goal that will help you change your writing behavior. Make it attainable, like writing for fifteen minutes a day. Find a quiet place or a place where you can tune out noise and simply write. Be intentional in recognizing your feelings about the process, and maybe make notes about your changing views of you as a writer.

Just dive in; problem solved. Sounds easy, right?

This exercise is an activity I use in my writing seminars. I'll be honest: some of the most confident teachers get nervous when faced with the prospect of staring down their past and spending time doing what they fear they cannot do. Don't be surprised if you experience a wide range of emotions—the frustration, anger, and shame that come through in other teachers' stories of their writing experiences. After you've come to terms with your history, pay attention to how your views on writing change. You may have a revelation related to a writing technique while waiting at a red light. An idea for a story will bloom in your mind while you're sweeping the floor. Your own writing may provide a good example you'll share with your students the next day. Writing may change from something you avoid at all costs to something you welcome. When this happens, you are thinking like a writer. You are a writer. And writers make the best writing teachers!

▍Busting Myths

Through talking with writing teachers at all levels, some themes that sound a whole lot like myths emerge. As you examine your own thoughts, you may find that you have some preconceived notions about writing, writing instruction, and writing teachers.

Myth 1: Good writing arrives on doves' wings.

In her book *In the Middle*, Nancie Atwell describes watching Donald Murray model his writing process in front of a group of teachers. She realizes that beautiful writing doesn't just "show up" and float from Murray's pen; writing is messy and difficult, and no one, authors included, has the luxury of perfect words simply falling from the sky. She exposes the misperception that writing "arrives on the wings of a dove."

The writing process is messy, and it's supposed to be that way. All children deserve to know and understand that writers aren't some privileged group with a direct line to the writing gods. They struggle and cross things out and rip up pages and get frustrated just like anyone else who has put pen to paper. Writers have also experienced that incredible feeling when they've made the words work, creating meaning that is clear and deep.

It's easy to picture someone like Ernest Hemingway or Virginia Woolf writing and believe their work must have been perfect on their very first drafts. Logically, that makes no sense. Great writers make great writing *look* easy; they are part wordsmith and part magician, making it appear that all the work going into writing was never there. In a way, that's a shame: think of the false impressions this creates for young writers and struggling writers. We should tell kids, "Your draft is looking sloppy? Well, it's supposed to be! That's how writing works!" or "You're stuck? All writers get stuck! Welcome to the club! Now, what can we do about it?"

Somehow, we've come to believe the opposite of perfection is failure, that if at first we don't succeed, we're doomed. Expecting perfect writing, especially in the early stages of the writing process, is dangerous. Perfection stops us from trying. Save perfection for final drafts and publishing. We cannot perpetuate the myth that good writing just happens magically.

> **Somehow, we've come to believe the opposite of perfection is failure, that if at first we don't succeed, we're doomed. Expecting perfect writing, especially in the early stages of the writing process, is dangerous. Perfection stops us from trying.**

What does this mean for you as a middle school writing teacher?

Look at your experiences, and examine your feelings about writing and perfection. Do you expect your writing to be perfect the first time around? Does writing something that really makes no sense at all seem like a waste to you?

I encourage you to let go and just write. If what you write works, great; if not, move on. Not every word put on paper is going to change the world. Write enough of those words and you'll come up with a nugget or two that might lead to something monumental. Writers keep writing notebooks. Not everything they write ends up being published. Give yourself permission to let words flow, and quit looking for those blasted doves. They don't exist. (If you'll do this, I'll go stick plants in the ground and not let my palms sweat. Honest.)

Challenge 1

Write each day. Write about washing dishes, walking your dog, getting to know your students. Write about things you remember from your childhood. Write about what makes you laugh, what makes you cry. When you're ready, take a line or two you've written, something that really speaks to you, and explore it. Use that idea as a springboard to something larger. By doing this you are learning to trust yourself to choose worthy topics.

> You can assure your students of the inevitability of bumps in the road and help them over those bumps because you've encountered the same obstacles. Your experiences pave the way for their experiences.

You are also giving yourself permission to stomp around in a topic and get knee-deep in the ever-messy writing process. Keep the importance of thought, the importance of telling a story in mind, leaving perfection and final drafts for much later. Beginning with a glimmer of an idea and making it into something that can be read and understood by others is a process you must live through to teach it to your students. You can assure your students of the inevitability of bumps in the road and help them over those bumps because you've encountered the same obstacles. Your experiences pave the way for their experiences.

Myth 2: The best writing teachers have finished their writing education—they know everything there is to know about writing.

We enter this profession with an anxiety that, if we think about it logically, is quite unrealistic. In our minds, we think everyone—kids, parents, fellow teachers, administrators—expects us to know everything there is to know about teaching and learning. Yet how can that be possible? We're inexperienced, right out of college. It takes years of practice to even feel the slightest glimmer of mastery in teaching. We are in a constant state of learning-by-doing.

I remember this perceived pressure well; my solution was to appear perfect. These children have one seventh-grade year, I thought, and if I am ineffective and lacking knowledge, that can't be fair. I preserved that image of sainthood at all costs. In writing, I assigned paragraphs (topics chosen by *moi*), used drill-and-kill worksheets on pronouns, and required essays so narrow in scope that I was sure I was providing students with everything they needed in writing instruction. It was exhausting—and despite my unending efforts, their writing was lousy.

The worst thing you can do as a writing teacher is claim you know it all; the next worst is to *think* you need to know it all. No teacher graduates from university with all the writing education she needs. Is this realistic for any profession? Does a doctor who performed knee surgery in 1976 continue to make these repairs in the same way today? We want the doctors who seek out the best techniques, the doctors who are open to new research and the best possible treatments. We want our doctors to be *students* of medicine, because someone who is always learning is always improving. The end result with these surgeries is the same: a repaired knee. However, we know the journey is just as important as the destination.

The great sculptors of the world don't claim to know every chip in the stone they'll make as they create masterpieces. Sculptors are students of their craft; they've studied, practiced, failed, created beauty, and considered the work of others. They've been inspired; they've also been devoid of creativity and felt the intense desire to chuck their mallets and chisels out the window. They are smart enough to know that within their ideas there are all kinds of variables. They know that in the beginning they do not have all the answers but that some will be revealed in the process of creation. This is true in writing as well. Writers begin with an idea. Some outline and plan thoroughly, but they'd be foolish not to stray from their original ideas when golden opportunities present themselves.

> The great sculptors of the world don't claim to know every chip in the stone they'll make as they create masterpieces....They are smart enough to know that within their ideas there are all kinds of variables."

How different your writing instruction will be when you tell yourself you don't know everything there is to know about writing and never will. You'll become much kinder to yourself. The process will become just as important as the product. You'll find joy in the journey and then pride in the finished work.

You'll become a better writer and a much better writing teacher. When you give yourself permission to be a student of writing, your focus shifts, and you open yourself up to the possibilities. Freed from the parameters of writing curriculums or writing programs, you'll be able to look at writing instruction through the eyes of someone who is learning. You start to show your students your drafts, soliciting their comments and advice. Can you imagine what it does for a student writer when his teacher says, "Gosh, I hadn't thought of that! What a great connection your idea creates in my piece. May I use that?" You've established yourself as someone who is in the middle of the struggle. You've shown that writing is a process, that your drafts get messy, and that you benefit when other eyes and minds consider your work.

An interesting contradiction presents itself here: claiming yourself as a student of writing does not mean throwing away your skills and knowledge. Don't make the mistake of confusing your role as a student of the craft with oh-heck-class-I-have-no-idea-what-I'm-doing-here-let's-just-write-endless-stories-and-call-it-good. Or better yet, let's-just-practice-the-life-out-of-prompt-writing-and-call-it-getting-ready-for-the-state-test (who can question preparing for the state exams?). As a middle school writing teacher, you must establish yourself as an authority. You must demonstrate that you know what middle school writers need and then be able to provide the lessons that are natural and useful for where they are developmentally. Matsuo Bashō, the father of haiku, wrote of this strange combination of behaviors in his work. He never claimed to know everything there was to know about haiku, yet his students knew he was the authority. Late in his life he wrote, "A caterpillar/this deep in fall—/still not a butterfly."

Maintaining this balance is no different than anything else you tackle in middle school. While the idea presents a challenge, take comfort that you already know what middle school writers need: the same things you need. Future chapters devoted to creating the environment middle school writers need and accompanying students on the journey deal with the nitty-gritty. All you have to do right now is work on your view of yourself as a writer and a writing teacher; the rest will make sense as your outlook evolves.

> **Your students are looking to you for guidance, but they also want to see your authenticity. Any teacher claiming to know it all doesn't.**

What does this mean to you as a middle school writing teacher?

Your students are looking to you for guidance, but they also want to see your authenticity. Any teacher claiming to know it all doesn't. With arrogance comes aloofness, and middle schoolers can spot a phony at ten desk lengths. Creating a know-it-all barrier around yourself does nothing for you, and it certainly will not make your students better writers. Be real, be authentic, and be willing to call yourself a student of writing. If you'll claim your status as a student and then truly begin to live as a student of writing, your world as a writing teacher will blossom. Your middle school students deserve this, and so do you!

Challenge 2

Concentrate on the ways you talk about writing with your students. The next time you present a writing lesson, make new statements to your students. When a child says she's stuck, read her work and say, "Hmm. I'm not sure what to do here. What have you considered doing to solve this?" Then listen intently. Other phrases you might use are:

» "Wow, I love that line! I wish I'd written that!"

» "This is very interesting. Where will this piece go next?"

» "I had this same problem in a story I wrote last month. Let me show you what I did, and then you can decide what to do from there."

» "I'm not sure about that. I'll think and you think, and let's meet in five minutes to see what we come up with."

By changing the way you talk to your students about writing, you are demonstrating problem solving, extending opportunities for you and your students to collaborate as writers, and establishing yourself as someone who is a student of *and* an authority on writing. Listen to your students' questions and learn to love them. Draw on your own writing experiences when you offer suggestions. If you don't know, say, "I don't know," but promise to think about it. You'll be amazed at what a change in your perspective will do to your writing classroom.

> **Draw on your own writing experiences when you offer suggestions. If you don't know, say, "I don't know," but promise to think about it.**

Myth 3: Teachers can fake their way through teaching writing to their students.

I've had many teachers tell me that of course they teach writing—their students are writing all the time. They write book reports and stories and responses to pieces of literature. They write letters to their second-grade buddies, they write long-answer responses on tests, and they practice for state evaluations until their fingers bleed.

It's really easy to confuse activity with instruction, especially if this describes our own writing experiences as children. Having students write is not delivering deliberate writing instruction. Assigning writing tasks and giving students grades for their stories is not teaching writing. Passing out worksheets so students can under-line prepositional phrases is an activity, not instruction.

> **It's really easy to confuse activity with instruction, especially if this describes our own writing experiences as children.**

Teaching writing requires more than keep-ing kids busy. Middle schoolers will not become better writers just by writing essay after essay. Practice does indeed make perfect, but without deliberate instruction, carefully chosen lessons, time spent talking about writing with others, and meaningful feedback from an instructor, our students will never realize their full potential as writers.

There's nothing I can do about my first years as a teacher, when I faked my way through teaching writing and substituted activity for instruction. What I can do is take a stance and move toward true writing instruction, in which students choose their topics, lessons are based on what mid-dle school writers need, and feedback is genuine, honest, helpful, and encouraging.

What does this mean to you as a middle school writing teacher?

Take an honest look at where you are and what writing instruction looks like in your classroom. Keep in mind that change is never easy. Be kind to yourself, and realize that as we grow and experience, we all become better.

Challenge 3

As you read the next few chapters, vow to keep an open mind. Sometimes "Oh, that will never work in my classroom" is a cover for "I'm scared as heck to make changes in what I do!" Remember that your job as a teacher is to do what is best for your students, not what is best for you. While I don't expect you to make this book your curriculum (far from it), please remain open to the possibilities presented, no matter how foreign they may seem.

Myth 4: I'll be a great writing teacher when the perfect writing curriculum comes along.

Marketing fascinates me. Currently, as our nation becomes more environmentally aware, I'm noticing how many businesses and manufacturers are professing their "green" practices and products. While I'm thrilled that people are making the effort to recycle, use less, and conserve our resources, watching businesses and corporations capitalize on what they see as a trend is a bit disheartening.

Not long ago, I got a flier in my box at school advertising WRITING WORKSHOP in big, bold letters. If I attended a seminar in a nearby city and paid my $250, I'd learn the secrets to teaching WRITING WORKSHOP. The price for the seminar included a notebook with all the worksheets I'd ever need to teach WRITING WORKSHOP. I tossed the flier into the recycling bin. Another case of marketing the life out of what someone perceives to be the next big trend.

Writing workshop is not a curriculum; it is an idea, a framework, a way of looking at how writing instruction should take place. There is no set curriculum; writing instruction in my classroom looks different from writing instruction in my teaching partner's room. We have the same beliefs, and we both embrace the tenets of writing workshop. We present the same topics, but how we get there is sometimes vastly different. Thinking there is one way to teach writing is preposterous!

If you're waiting for the perfect curriculum to make you a fantastic writing teacher, you're going to wait a long time—forever, in fact. Writing is too personal, too personalized to the needs of the kids you have each year. No suggested approach, no matter how complete or neat or tidy, can give you everything you need. Several professional books, written by writing teachers I admire, are always within my reach. As comprehensive as their lessons are, simply duplicating them, page after page, is not going to make me the best writing

> **Writing instruction is a compilation of your own experiences, the wisdom of others, and what your students tell you and show you they need.**

teacher ever, nor will is give my students the rich, individualized experiences they need. Writing instruction is a compilation of your own experiences, the wisdom of others, and what your students tell you and show you they need.

What does this mean to you as a middle school writing teacher?

The way toward becoming the writing teacher that all children deserve lies within you, not in a textbook or a canned program. While published materials support some aspects of writing, what you bring to your young writers makes the bigger impact.

Challenge 4

For the next few days, pay specific attention to your needs as a writing teacher. Keep in mind that you, not a prepackaged lesson or program, drive instruction. Be as honest as possible as you answer the following questions:

1. What are your current fears relative to writing instruction? What are their origins? What can you do to get past them?
2. What are your strongest abilities related to teaching writing? (Don't list your best lessons or assignments. List the strengths you bring to instruction.)
3. What do you want your students to know and practice before your time with them is through?
4. What and who will help you grow into the best writing teacher you can be?
5. Are there others willing to embark on this journey with you? How can you invite them along?

You make writing instruction happen in your classroom. Your willingness to develop your own talents as a writer and a writing teacher will pave the way for your middle school writers. Your impact is enormous; your input and wisdom are vital. This responsibility is a bit frightening, but it is exciting too. You are about to create amazing experiences for your writing students!

3

Strengthening Your Confidence

Planning an Environment for Young Writers

AS A YOUNG ADULT, I had the good fortune to work as a counselor at a sleep-away camp. While not the job to take if one needs serious cash, to this day I maintain that I discovered more about teaching and learning there than in all four years of my undergraduate teacher training. Besides learning how to function on little sleep, use the materials on hand, and keep large groups of children on task and moving forward (sound familiar?), I realized that I had to create an experience for the children in my care. They had one week at camp out of an entire summer. If they were anything like I was as a child, they spent a whole lot of time during the winter dreaming about those precious seven days. They could have the most amazing week with me, or camp could be just okay.

I could gently nudge the campers to try new outdoor cooking methods, or they could eat hot dogs cooked over an open fire for the seventh summer in a row. I could teach them how to paddle a canoe using clear instruction, positive reinforcement, and helpful tips, or I could hand them a paddle, send them out on the lake, and hope they figured out the difference between a J stroke and a C stroke. As a counselor, I used my past experiences to guide, cajole, insist, demonstrate, model, evaluate, and reteach if needed. If a camper couldn't get the hang of a knot she was learning to tie, I'd never say, "Well, I guess you're just not cut out for knot tying." I'd find another way to teach her, show her again; everyone was capable of greatness.

My camp experiences had a huge impact on how I approach teaching writing. I realize that students in my class can walk away in June not only as skilled writers but also as people who are excited to write. They can try what I place before them and achieve lots more than they ever thought possible, or they can finish the year feeling just as ambivalent as they did when they walked through the door in September. My choices and approaches create opportunities for success—or not.

The same idea applies to school. What happens in a classroom must be centered on the needs of students. The learning that takes place needs to produce skilled writers who understand audience, voice, and the approaches one should use for different writing situations. We need to produce confident writers who, when faced with difficult writing tasks, may not know how to begin but have the skills and perseverance to find the way.

> **What happens in a classroom must be centered on the needs of students.**

We need to produce writers who understand that writing is thinking, and who see writing as a path to communication, a way to share knowledge, and an opportunity to be creative and produce something from nothing. *How* our students learn to approach writing, now and in the future, is up to us. We are the catalyst for that change.

I don't know about you, but this both frightens and fuels me.

DIGGING DEEPER

1. How are my students changed by the experiences they have in my classroom?
2. What are one or two things I want them to take away from my class when they leave me?

▌ Creating the Environment

Middle school writers need an environment that is designed for their success. Within that place, certain conditions must exist to create a system that works smoothly and gives students the best chances for writing growth. Some of these conditions have to do with what you'll offer students, like control of the choices they'll make in their writing. Others have to do with the structures within your classroom, like setting up the daily routine and teaching the processes you want students to utilize. Yet others have to do with how you'll foster relationships within your classroom, beginning with you as a compassionate demander and how students will come to know each other to build a safe and supportive writing community. These elements, working in harmony, become the environment that all middle schoolers need to reach their full potential as writers.

▮ Charting Your Course: Choosing Choice

As a writing teacher, allowing student choice costs nothing yet yields benefits beyond measure. You can read all kinds of research and opinions about the impact choice has in educating students, but choice is essential in creating successful and skillful writers, especially at the middle level. Offering choice is how to get kids to write.

In your definition of choice, be open to letting students choose what is important to them as their topics for writing. Plenty of teachers say they give their students choice in their writing—"I give them two prompts, and they get to choose the one they want to respond to"—but the choice is minimal at best. The children are still expected to write about what the teacher wants them to write about. This kind of choice is minimal and does not allow kids to begin the process of taking control of their work.

Giving up control is not easy for teachers. The nature of our daily job demands control. We are sitting ducks, outnumbered thirty (or more) to one. Without control, our lives at school would be one exercise in frustration after another. We are used to stepping up, taking charge, dictating what needs to be done, where it needs to be done, and when it needs to be done. We know that without

> Giving up control is not easy for teachers. The nature of our daily job demands control. . . . Nevertheless, we need to examine the idea of control in our writing instruction.

our being in control, our students will never learn to function in a classroom, never make the academic progress needed to move on to the next grade. We know the importance of schedules, of processes, of systems. We know how to make the best use of our thirty-minute lunch periods: we confer with a student, make copies, use the restroom, check in with colleagues, *and* eat. We are the epitome of self-discipline and control!

Nevertheless, we need to examine the idea of control in our writing instruction. We assign writing prompts for a number of reasons. First, we're afraid kids won't know what to write about and will end up just sitting there, trying to come up with a topic—and we hate wasting time. Second, we know what the state tests look like—and giving students writing prompts that look like state writing assessment prompts will make them better at taking the tests, right? Third, the only writing instruction most of us have ever known involved writing about the topics our teachers gave us. If it worked for us, it should work for our students. (But truthfully, did it really work for us?) Finally, assigning writing topics is a way to make sure all our students get the same writing experiences. They all read the same paragraphs in the social studies book. They all do the same lab assignments in science. Why shouldn't kids all have the same writing topics? Let's deal with these arguments one at a time.

Kids won't know what to write about.

True. If we leave topic choice up to kids whose writing experiences up to that point have been triggered by teacher-driven prompts, most of them won't have a clue what to write about. Why should they? They've grown accustomed to being spoon-fed topics and are quite comfortable not having to think much. Who wouldn't become alarmed if suddenly a teacher said, "No, I'm not assigning your writing topics; you're choosing your own!" If we leave it there, yes, we'll find a lot of kids sitting at desks and staring off into space.

But kids can learn how to choose their own topics. We can talk about how writers find topics for stories, poems, and novels and teach them to create their own writing "territories" (Atwell 1998) or "authorities" (Fletcher and Portalupi 2004). We can show students our writing territories and give them time to create their own, listing possible topics in their writing notebook, keeping it close at hand for inspiration, and adding more possibilities as the year progresses. When a student tells you she doesn't know what to write about, respond with, "What do you think you should do about that?" and remind her about the list of topics in her writing notebook. This redirection helps students remember that stash of ideas they compiled, just waiting to be explored for possible stories and poems.

Offering choice can be tricky. Some teachers are comfortable letting their students choose both genre and topic. Others have a difficult time giving up either decision. My experience with middle school writers is that many of them are not willing to venture outside their comfort zones. As their teacher, I also know they need exposure to and success in all kinds of genres. The compromise that works best for my students and me is for the students to have full control of their topic choices, while I decide the genres we explore in class. Your practice will become more comfortable with experience. Begin where you feel confident, pay attention to how your students deal with choice, and make any necessary adjustments.

Writing to prompts helps kids do well on state tests.

There is no question that high-stakes testing has made its way into our classrooms, schools, and districts. Seventh grade is a reporting year in our state, and my school's scores are published in the newspaper for all to see. I know that the numbers in print are only one aspect of the data collected and that peeling back the layers of information reveals different views of progress (or lack of it). However, all that seems to matter is the percentage of students meeting standards—and how that number compares with last year, for different kids! Naturally, we do what we've always done when requirements are imposed on us: we teach the heck out of whatever will be evaluated so that we pass.

Most of us played "school" really well as kids. We did what our teachers asked and did it well. And we still feel that need to please. We make sure students know that in a five-paragraph essay there is an introduction (to include a hook and a thesis statement), three supporting body paragraphs, and a conclusion. We make sure they understand transitions, order of importance, and how to use solid, logical arguments to persuade. Formal essays certainly have their place in a writing program. However, if students leave us thinking that the five-paragraph essay, in persuasive and expository forms, is the *only* type of writing out there, we've done them a huge disservice. If test preparation is the only writing instruction students receive, they miss out on all the other kinds of writing (and the amazing techniques and structures students can learn by writing poetry and fiction and memoir and biography). Strictly test writing provides students with a limited view of composition, and that's not fair.

What worked for us should work for our students.

Everyone who becomes a teacher has spent thousands of hours observing teachers. From the age of five we've watched as teachers instructed, disciplined, and supervised. We go into the teaching profession having a pretty good idea of what teachers do, at least when it comes to being in the classroom. I'm hard-pressed to think of another profession that affords that much exposure prior to formal training.

> **Everyone who becomes a teacher has spent thousands of hours observing teachers. . . . When at a loss, it is easy to fall back on what we know.**

When at a loss, it is easy to fall back on what we know. You may have, on occasion, asked yourself how your own teachers presented materials or taught lessons. If our own writing instruction consisted of prompts, story starters, and other writing activities designed by the teacher, we may feel the need to carry on the tradition. But our students deserve better writing instruction than we got as kids.

Assigning writing topics ensures that everyone makes the same progress.

Historically, we've had the mistaken belief that if all kids follow the same instructions and have the same writing experiences, they will all make the same progress in becoming better writers. But writing is not a content discipline; it is a process. Kids thrive when their writing instruction is tailored to them. Not all children enter the classroom with the same writing skills. Some will be writing like adults, some like much younger students, some not at all. Giving a prompt to a group of students with varied skills and abilities meets the needs of only a few. The rest will be either bored or

> **Kids thrive when their writing instruction is tailored to them.**

totally confused. The results we hope to achieve by giving all students the same writing activity won't materialize. A prompt about having $100 to spend at the mall won't spark the imagination of a kid who hates to shop. Writing a story about what would happen if students sprouted wings may seem ridiculous to half the class. Students who play by the rules will do the work. Some of the students who think the prompt is a waste of time will write, but the effort they expend will be minimal at best. Others won't write at all.

The way to engage every writer in your classroom is to allow for the variety that student choice provides. We put more effort into what we believe is important. That's true for kids as well as adults. When we own something, it becomes personal.

DIGGING DEEPER

1. How does this idea of giving students topic and/or genre choice strike me?
2. How much student choice do I incorporate into my school day? Where do I offer students choice?
3. What are two or three doable ways I might incorporate student choice into my day right now?

Preparing the Schedule: Giving Students a Routine They Can Count On

Part of feeling safe is knowing what to anticipate. While I'm not one for hard-core, inflexible schedules, I do believe that a structural pattern within a class period is a form of comfort for middle school students. This structure also guides my instruction and reminds me to stay true to my ideals.

There are millions of ways to structure your day. Whatever the plan, the outcome is the same: a daily progression of events that your students can more or less count on. I'll share what works best for me; maybe you'll find it works for you too, or maybe you'll modify it. My typical class period plays out like this:

1. **Greetings.** My first greeting is at the door during the transition between classes. I shake hands with each student and say, "Hi! How are you today?" (We practice this at the beginning of the school year and talk about shaking hands, making eye contact, and giving a response.) After morning announcements (if it's the first class of the day) or the bell, students know their attention is to be on me (a taught behavior). I am sincere when I begin class with "Good morning" or "Good afternoon," to which my students respond in kind. I then say something like "Welcome back!" or "Good to see you all!" or "I thought of you all this weekend when . . . ." I utter some variation of these words every day, because I *am* glad to see them. I want them to feel welcome in a place in which they truly belong.

2. **Roll question** (five to ten minutes). Each class begins with a new question and a chance to get to know one another better. This is one of my favorite times of the day! (See the in-depth discussion of this practice at the end of this chapter.)

3. **Journal writing** (five minutes). This is a warm-up. At the beginning of the year I ask students what they do if they want to get better at something, like making free throws or riding a skateboard. We talk about the purpose of practice and how it is no different with writing. Practice makes better writers, and writing in their journal is a chance to practice. I never assign journal topics, just as I never assign writing topics. Students are free to write whatever they choose. Some students use their journal as a diary, keeping track of their day-to-day lives. Others use it as an outlet for their emotions. Some write poetry; others spend the year writing an ongoing story. I don't read these journals (unless students ask me to) or grade them. I do give daily points for having a journal and writing in it. I try my best to write along with the class. Students need to see me doing what I expect them to do. Besides, any chance I have to write is a good thing!

4. **Vocabulary instruction** (three to five minutes). Each week my students are introduced to a new root word and five words that use that root. I teach root words common in various disciplines so that

students have the building blocks to make educated guesses when they encounter new terms.

5. **Minilesson** (five to ten minutes). These short, focused lessons directly apply to students' current writing. Minilessons are covered in-depth in the next chapter.

6. **Work/conferences on current project** (twenty minutes). I move around the room, answering questions and meeting with writers one-on-one or in small groups. Students work silently, and the conversations I have with them are whispered. I expect this time to be productive, never wasted (an expectation I address at the beginning of the year; it won't just happen on its own).

7. **Sharing** (brief and informal, as time permits). This part of the class is essential for creating a community. Students have an opportunity to share something they wrote that they feel is particularly good. I ask for volunteers. As students become more comfortable with their classmates and their own writing, the number of volunteers increases. It's not long before a chorus of disappointment sounds when I announce we have time for only one more share. (Sometimes a student will ask in advance to read something to the class. I always make time for these brave souls.)

8. **Parting words** (one minute). I remind students about deadlines and about what they'll need for class tomorrow and wish them a good rest of the day.

We all feel pressure, each and every day, to get everything done, but flexibility is the name of the game. If there isn't time to share at the end a period, the world won't end. On days when peer writing groups meet or we hold an "open mic," journal writing and vocabulary instruction go out the window. If I'm really feeling pressed for time, I'll forego the roll question. (But students invariably put up a fight!) Make time work for you—don't be a slave to it. And take comfort in the fact that since you've taught procedures ahead of time and created a safe haven for your students, you won't spend as much time correcting inappropriate behavior—there'll be very little of it!

You will always be able to teach more with fewer distractions if you take the time to prepare a safe place for your middle school writers.

DIGGING DEEPER

1. What does/might a schedule in my classroom look like?
2. If I follow a schedule, are there ways to tweak it to make it even more efficient?
3. If I don't follow a schedule, how would instituting one impact my day-to-day teaching?

Preparing Yourself: Becoming the Teacher All Kids Deserve

We middle school teachers walk a fine line. We must have high standards for work and behavior yet still be flexible and caring. We have to know when it's okay to bird-walk a bit and when we have to stay on track. We need to know when it's okay to laugh so hard we cry and when it's time to be serious. This constant state of evaluation is dizzying for most folks. Those of us who teach middle school know that our survival depends on this skill.

Two words that normally don't go together create the perfect descriptor for someone possessing this ability: *compassionate demander*. Let's examine this label.

> **Compassion in the classroom is perceiving or being aware of an entire person or an entire situation. A compassionate teacher understands that life happens.**

The word *compassionate* conjures up visions of care. A compassionate person is aware of the others in his presence. *Understanding* is the synonym most people would attach to the word *compassionate*, but in this instance, it goes beyond that. Compassion in the classroom is perceiving or being aware of an entire person or an entire situation. A compassionate teacher understands that life happens. Wednesday evening's homework takes a back burner when a pet has to be rushed to the vet. A student who is distracted and scattered because her grandma is in the hospital needs to be cut some slack. A compassionate teacher realizes that outside forces have an impact on what goes on in her classroom and that trying to pretend that stress, crisis, and loss can be left at the door is shortsighted. A compassionate middle school teacher also understands how social, academic, physical, and emotional development impacts the students in her care. She understands that the giant pimple on a boy's face can cause him to check out of her lesson on possessive nouns. When she sees a girl in the back sneaking looks at her hair in a compact mirror, she remembers what it was like to be an eighth grader worried about how others see her. Compassionate correction and redirection is swift, sure, and gentle. The compassionate teacher has no need to humiliate or demean; she knows that every behavior has a reason, and she doesn't take personally things most people would consider disrespectful. She sees intervening in less-than-positive behavior not as an opportunity to impose consequences but as a chance for students to learn something—about themselves, about being human, about growing up a little.

The term *demander* connotes someone with drive, someone who has a goal in mind and knows what to do to achieve it. People describe their parents, their bosses, and their teachers as demanding. Power is established in this term: one person is making—sometimes forcing—another person do something. A demander is not always seen in a positive light; pushing for compliance often leads to conflict. The person of whom an action is demanded may feel powerless, but the demander sees the task as vital to the goal. Teachers who are demanders are described as strict, straightforward, and no-nonsense. While these are not bad qualities, we've all had teachers who were abrupt in their instruction and interactions. Demanders know what is right, end of story. Demanders don't always let their feelings toward others show for fear that progress might be stalled by all that "touchy-feely interpersonal stuff." Achievement is most important, and demanders know how to get there.

Pairing *compassionate* and *demander* is an interesting juxtaposition, and it certainly describes teaching middle school. These seemingly polar opposites form a perfectly beautiful title for the best middle school teachers on the planet. So what does a compassionate demander as a middle school writing teacher look like? Here she is in action!

A compassionate demander knows that corrective confrontation is sometimes necessary but that it should not be demeaning or discouraging.

She knows how things should happen in her classroom but understands that middle school kids are sometimes unpredictable. When issues arise, she:

» Addresses the problem in a timely manner.

» Corrects behavior quietly or in private whenever possible.

» Works with students to find a way to solve the problem.

How this works in real life. While my students are working on final drafts in the computer lab, I notice Bob talking animatedly to his neighbor. When I remind him that this is not okay, he rolls his eyes and says, "Whatever." I pull him aside and, rather than lecture, ask, "Are you okay? You seem a little off today." Bob has clearly expected to be reprimanded and looks surprised. He tells me he is tired and having a horrible day. I say I'm sorry things are bad, but this doesn't mean he has to make bad choices in class. He immediately volunteers, "I think I'll move to another computer so I'm not tempted to talk to Michael." All that remains is for me to give him a pat on the back and say (with a smile), "Good decision."

The outcome. Both Bob and I come away from the confrontation feeling positive. Bob has been empowered to take charge of his own behavior and will, I hope, internalize the idea that he can make positive choices, no matter how his day is going. He realizes I care about both how his life is going and his progress and productivity in class.

The compassionate demander keeps the student's whole life in mind when considering behavior that doesn't match her expectations.

She understands that students are sometimes powerless in their nonschool lives, and if a parent requires an older student to babysit his younger siblings until 10 p.m. on Tuesday night, the homework turned in on Wednesday morning may not be complete or of high quality. She:

» Talks with the student to find out why the work is perfunctory or incomplete.

> » Listens carefully to see whether the "more" to the story requires the assistance of a school counselor or community professional.
> » Sets a new deadline and a plan for the work to get done—having a working lunch in the classroom, staying after school, or going to the library during study hall.

How this works in real life. When I don't receive the assigned final draft from Cheryl, I'm surprised. She's very reliable about turning in her work, so I'm a little shocked when she tells me it's not done. I always check in with kids who don't meet a deadline, and I ask her to stay after class. The tears start before she makes it to the front of the room. I ask what's going on, and she says her older brother was in a motorcycle accident the night before. While her parents were at the hospital, she babysat her younger siblings and her brother's daughters. She tried to work on her final draft, but it was too hard to concentrate with the little kids around and the worry she felt for her brother. She did stay up late typing the piece, but then realized her printer was out of ink. After verifying that her brother is going to be okay, I say, "You know what? Life happens. Last night was obviously out of your control. How about we set a new deadline?" I also remind her that she can email the final draft to me if getting ink for the printer in the next few days is impossible.

The outcome. Cheryl feels cared about. She's learned that sometimes adjustments must be made to accommodate the unexpected events in life and that flexibility in these situations is more likely because of her past responsible behavior. Her stress is relieved because she can finish her task without penalty. I get a chance to support her, and I make sure to ask about her brother until he's well on his way to being fully healed.

A compassionate demander has a keen sense for deciphering excuses.

She is willing to err on the side of caution when evaluating reasons for incomplete work but is keenly aware when a pattern of unfinished tasks is established. She realizes when a student has cried wolf one too many times. She:

> » Meets with the student to talk about the pattern of excuses she has observed.

» Asks, "Has turning work in on time been a recurring problem for you?"

» When it is apparent that the late work is a result of poor planning and misused time, reminds the student that deadlines are sacred and important.

» Works through two situations with the student:

> When the current missing work will be turned in.

> How to avoid missing deadlines in the future.

» May decide to contact the student's parents and let them know about the missing work.

» Doesn't take the situation personally, instead realizes that this is a chance for the student to grow up a little and take more responsibility.

How this works in real life. Sarah joins my class midyear and doesn't fully understand the seriousness of missing a deadline. When I confront her, she makes light of the situation, saying with a chuckle, "To be honest, I haven't turned in a completed writing assignment for the last two years." When I ask why, she shrugs her shoulders. I ask how her former teachers reacted to this. Another shrug. I tell her that not turning in work is a problem in my class, that I expect 100 percent of my students to turn in 100 percent of their assignments. I gently but firmly say this is her chance to grow up a bit and take charge of her learning. She remains aloof as we arrange a new due date. When she misses the new deadline, I email her parents. Although most parents respond to such a message, I hear nothing from hers. This signals me that for Sarah, school needs to happen at school. I require working lunches until the writing is finished. After two weeks of these lunches, the writing "gets lost." Since there has to be something else going on, I ask Sarah, "I want you to be unfailingly honest with me. What is stopping you from completing your work?" She takes a second and says, "Two things. I have ADHD, and my parents can't afford the medication right now. And I think I'm a really bad writer." I acknowledge the difficulties that ADHD presents and ask what we can do to address the "bad writer" perception. When she doesn't answer, I ask whether she's comfortable letting me read something she's written, anything, so I can assess her work. She reluctantly gives me a poem she's written—on her own! It's a pretty amazing poem for a thirteen-year-old girl, and I tell her so. Although turning in work continues to be a struggle, she turns in the last two projects of the year on time.

The outcome. Sarah and I both learn lessons on perseverance and problem solving. Sarah gains confidence in her writing ability and eventually changes her behavior. She also learns that I'm paying attention and am not reluctant to contact her parents. (They didn't respond until the missing work resulted in a midterm failing grade.) I hope Sarah has also learned that facing a problem head-on is always better than ignoring it and that it's okay to ask for help. In any case, she now realizes that success resides in her hands—and yes, she has grown up a little!

A compassionate demander understands that she may be one of the few steady adults in her students' lives—that her students see her as a lifeline.

She knows that middle school kids aren't always the picture of tact and sometimes share information at the most inopportune times—in the middle of a lesson, perhaps. When a student blurts out that her grandmother has died, for example, she:

- » Realizes that the seriousness of the announcement cannot be ignored.
- » Gives the student a few moments to talk, even though the class is in the middle of a lesson.
- » Knows the class doesn't find this odd, because the culture within the classroom puts people first. The students know the girl's grandma has been ill.
- » Takes a few moments to acknowledge the death and then says, "Can you stay after class for a bit so we can talk more?"

If the announcement made by the student is prosaic or inconsequential ("I got new shoes last night" or "My brother is grounded"), she gently shuts down the topic, reminding the student that a better time to talk is before or after class.

How this works in real life. In the middle of a lesson, Lynn raises her hand and says, "My dad wrote me a letter. I got it on Saturday." The class goes silent; they know Lynn hasn't had contact with her dad for most of her thirteen years. I say, "Really? That is huge. How are you feeling?" Lynn explains she's not sure. She feels abandoned and that makes her mad, but it's her dad, and she really wants to know him. After a moment of silence, a boy says: "I don't know how to react to that! I'm sorry you have to decide." The other kids nod and murmur their agreement. Before continuing the lesson, I ask Lynn if she'll see me before she goes to lunch. She does, filling in more details and reiterating how torn she feels. I remind her I'm here if she needs to talk and offer the services of the school counselor. During the remainder of the year, I ask Lynn how things are going and tell her I'm thinking about her and the decision she'll make.

The outcome. Lynn feels supported by her classmates, who have become like family. She knows there are plenty of people who will listen, whatever decision she makes.

What does being a compassionate demander have to do with the conditions in my writing class? *Everything.* As a compassionate demander, I am aware of everything that goes on. The classroom is not about me—it is about my students and their developing sense of themselves as writers. I think back to myself as a middle school student. I did a lot of observing and listening, trying to figure out how things worked. I observed whether my teachers were approachable. I listened to how instructors responded to other students' questions to determine whether my own questions would be met with dignity or scorn. I paid attention to what kinds of classroom managers my teachers were. Would they let counterproductive or mean-spirited behavior slide, or would they confront students who were inappropriate, making it quite clear that their actions were jeopardizing the safe environment for the other kids in class?

In short, students are watching carefully to see what they can expect. While they obviously don't know the term, the teacher they are looking for is a compassionate demander. Students want a teacher who is in charge but in a loving and respectful way. No matter what they tell you, students do not want chaos. A classroom that is out of control may feel familiar to students, but it does not feel good. They need and want someone who greets them at the

> **Students want a teacher who is in charge but in a loving and respectful way.**

door and says, "Good morning! How are you today?" They want a teacher who demands complete attention during lessons. There is safety in boundaries, and students need to know that when the expectations are not met, something is going to happen, whether it is a direct confrontation, a quiet conference, an after-class talking to, or a phone call home. Remember their battle cry of "That's not fair!"? Why not be the fairness they seek? Be willing to listen, but also be willing to step up and intervene when a student is acting inappropriately. Make your expectations clear, but understand that middle school kids mess up sometimes; it is not the end of the world nor an indication that society is going you-know-where in a handbasket.

Compassionate demanders are present in their classrooms, their eyes fixed on the end product, while at the same time acknowledging the importance of the journey, bumps and all. They are the hub of safety. They create that secure environment kids crave. Teachers who are compassionate demanders don't allow students to walk away from a class saying, "See, I told you. Teachers are all the same." By being a compassionate demander, we become more than a teacher to our students. Our predictable and steady behavior makes us safe adults. We not only guide our students through the writing process but also become the person they seek out when they need to talk, either about positive things or negative things.

> **By being a compassionate demander, we become more than a teacher to our students. Our predictable and steady behavior makes us safe adults.**

My teaching partner and I always joke about "the five-minute crises." At our school, students have five minutes to move from one class to another, and during those few moments of downtime, crises invariably bubble to the surface. We marvel at the situations we encounter:

>> "I think Kevin is cutting himself again."

>> "I forgot my project at home! What do I do?"

>> "I feel sick, can I—" followed by vomiting in the hallway.

>> "I lost my contact lens!"

>> "My dad got really mad at me last night."

>> "I'm grounded. Again."

» "What do you do if a friend tells you she's thinking about having sex with her boyfriend?"

» "I hate my math teacher. He's mean and totally unfair."

» "My mom kicked my brother out on Saturday."

» "I think I'm gay."

Becoming a compassionate demander makes you approachable, and as a result, students feel comfortable sharing the ups and downs of their lives with you. A relationship of trust develops, and an easy give-and-take exists because your classroom is a haven. Day-in and day-out existence becomes easier because they can count on being met with dignity and respect. Students can rely on you as a steady force (even on days when your own life outside school is hectic or falling apart). Because of that surety, that predictability, students can put aside their insecurities and the behavior that is often an attempt to mask them. There is little need to misbehave, because students feel comfortable in what they can expect. The sense of trust that develops assures them that you won't ask for busywork, that the writing tasks you present are necessary and useful. In turn, you'll expect that their writing will be high quality, done on deadline, and thoughtful. When it isn't, students can expect some kind of intervention, at school for sure and at home if necessary. A missing writing assignment does not go unnoticed, because your role as a compassionate demander doesn't allow it to be. Instead, you confer with the student, make a plan, call home to alert parents, and hold the student accountable. Through your actions, you're letting students know that your care for them does not allow you to allow them to fail. You'll stick by them in good times and bad, gently pushing them to be the best writers (and people!) they can be.

DIGGING DEEPER

Think about your last few years of teaching.

1. What are a few examples of my best compassionate demander moments? How did I feel about my students during those moments?

2. What about a time when I was out of balance? How did I feel about my students then?

3. How can striving to be a compassionate demander benefit my students *and* me?

4. Given my personality and teaching style, what are three changes I can make today that will help me become an even better compassionate demander than I already am?

Preparing Expectations: Teaching Processes Explicitly

Management is important in all classrooms. Any smart teacher thinks ahead and makes mental pictures of the classroom of her dreams. Middle school teachers need to take that mental picture one step further and predict the reactions and possible behavior that will be exhibited when parameters are established.

At the beginning of the school year, we are eager to begin academic work. In the drive to get going, we sometimes bypass teaching the behavior we wish to see exhibited in our classrooms. But there is nothing wrong with beginning a school year by thoroughly teaching classroom processes. Knowing what to do when is another element of students' sense of safety and security. Think how differently learning to drive a car would have been if our driver education instructor said, "Okay, get in, turn the key, and go," instead of explaining each step of the way as the needed skill presented itself.

Teaching important classroom behaviors not only saves our sanity but also creates the conditions our writers need to develop and grow. Well-established routines and processes allow us to spend less time redirecting undesirable behavior and more time working with students on their writing. We're able to pull a small group aside and work with them because the rest of the kids in the class know that when we are with a group, they're expected to attempt to solve their own problems. They know they should move on to another piece or another section of an essay instead of sitting and waiting. They know that when we work with an

> **Teaching important classroom behaviors not only saves our sanity but also creates the conditions our writers need to develop and grow.**

individual, the rest of the class is to continue working; they won't mistake unsupervised time as playtime.

Here's a list of possible things to teach at the beginning of the year:

1. How the class will begin and end.
2. How to salute the flag.
3. When it's okay to sharpen pencils, throw something away, and get out of your seat.
4. How to behave during roll question.
5. How to pass papers in (and out).
6. The signal for coming to attention.
7. How and when to ask questions in class.
8. How to behave during minilessons.
9. How to retrieve and put away writing notebooks.
10. How to behave during writing conferences.
11. How to behave when writing a draft.
12. How to participate in minilessons.
13. How to treat one another.
14. What to do if you've been absent.
15. What to do if you come to class late.
16. What to do if you are stuck in your writing.
17. What to do if you don't have supplies.
18. What to do if your projects and/or assignments are late.
19. How to get extra help.
20. What to do if someone is not treating you well.

Teach behavior up front and early so that you don't have to teach behavior all year long. Once you begin teaching not only *what* you want to happen in your classroom but also *how* you want it to happen, you'll find yourself with extra instructional time. Classes move faster and students do more writing because you won't have to stop and redirect behavior as frequently as you have in the past. You'll also be able to relax a bit as the year progresses, because you'll trust that your students know what to do and know that you expect them to do the right thing. While some might consider teaching procedures and behaviors "lost time," we who do so know that it gives us more time in the long run. On day 150 of the school year, we are not correcting behavior during class because our expectations were taught, corrected, and reinforced earlier in the year.

Do yourself a favor and slow down at the beginning of the school year. Visualize what you want to happen in your classroom, and identify the ways in which you'll share those expectations with your students. The benefits will far outweigh the effort and time.

DIGGING DEEPER

1. What behavior around process do I find myself correcting over and over again?
2. How can I address this behavior so it doesn't disrupt the teaching, learning, and work that take place in my classroom?

What happens and doesn't happen in your classroom is up to you. If students' behavior is not where you want it to be, you have the ability to make the changes necessary. If you are midyear, avoid an it's-a-new-day style overhaul. Start small, add on, and eventually you'll arrive in the place that feels right for you and your students. Next year, when it truly is a new day, teach processes explicitly, in full awareness that what you teach in the beginning makes your classroom a productive and comfortable place for an entire year.

Getting to Know Each Other: Becoming "Our Class"

Years ago I watched a television news show about middle school. The host of the program wanted to know what it was that made middle school one of life's nightmares. The people being interviewed were celebrities and people off the street alike. Men, women, old, young, they all said the same thing: middle school was a hell not to be repeated. They recounted

insecurities and fears about physical changes, belonging, peer relationships, boyfriends, girlfriends, embarrassing moments, and teachers.
While it's true that some of the changes in early adolescence cannot be
avoided, the social uncertainty can be cushioned by the actions of a per-
ceptive teacher.

Adolescent social posturing is swift and sure. Put thirty middle school
kids in one room, give them twenty minutes of unstructured time, and
groups will form. The pretty people will find the
other pretty people, the jocks will find the jocks.
The geeks will congregate, and the nerds may
draw together—or just keep reading their books.
Emily Dickinson wrote, "The soul selects her own
society then shuts the door," and nowhere is this
more evident than in middle school.

> **Emily Dickinson wrote, "The soul selects her own society then shuts the door," and nowhere is this more evident than in middle school.**

When groups are allowed to flourish, power
and domain are established and a hierarchy put
in place. There will always be those who domi-
nate and those who will be dominated. Whenever
exclusionary practices are allowed, getting to know those in other groups
is discouraged. A cafeteria in any secondary school illustrates this point
beautifully. Those in the lower social castes are not worthy; those in higher
castes are snobs, and fraternizing is discouraged.

There is a similar insecurity *within* cliques. Rather than take the chance
of being ostracized, group members refrain from taking risks, knowing full
well the wrath of the other members. Not wanting to experience the ridicule
inflicted on outsiders for their "weird" behavior, members remain silent to
preserve their status within the group.

If this microcosm is allowed in a classroom, a safe haven for writers will
never exist. A thirteen-year-old isn't going to volunteer to share what she or
he just wrote if the jocks are going to snicker and roll their eyes. Likewise,
one of the pretty people isn't going to read the poem she wrote about how
ugly she feels, inside and out. There is no safety in this situation.

So What Do We Do?

We begin by creating the proverbial level playing field. We don't allow
exclusion, because exclusion is not okay. We gently prod kids to get to know

one another—when you know someone, it's difficult to dismiss them with a sweeping generalization.

Given the social tendencies of middle schoolers, it seems ironic that we need to encourage our students to know one another. They may know how to be social on their terms, but I want my students also to be social on *my* terms. I want them to form a group called "our class." I want them to begin to feel that we, all of us, are part of something that transcends social cliques. I want them to understand that everyone has value and that everyone contributes to the rich culture we build through the year. I want them to know something about everyone.

What I'm about to share is the cornerstone of my teaching: my management booster, my lifeline, the means by which my classroom becomes a safe place for middle schoolers. All this power rests in the ritual my students and I perform at the start of each and every class: roll question. I ask my students a question at the start of every class. These questions are not academic and are not answered on paper with a pencil. They have nothing to do with finding the errors in a sentence written on the board. They are adolescent friendly, and every student has a chance to answer. They run the gamut from "If your favorite dessert were sitting on your desk right now, what would we see?" to "What do your siblings do to make you crazy?" to "What is the most difficult thing about being you?"

When I describe this practice to other teachers, many of them blow it off: "That sounds as if it takes a long time, and I don't have the time to lose. I have important things to teach, you know." I do know. I know we all feel crunched for time. I know the pressure we feel to make sure our students are making appropriate progress and achieving on those state tests. However, the message underlying these teachers' dismissal is, "I'm afraid

> **Given the social tendencies of middle schoolers, it seems ironic that we need to encourage our students to know one another. They may know how to be social on their terms, but I want my students also to be social on *my* terms.**

> **What I'm about to share is the cornerstone of my teaching. . . . I ask my students a question at the start of every class.**

to let my students know me." And that's why, while it does take time each day (sometimes more than I intend), I'll never stop asking the roll questions, because they make my classroom a place to belong. My students know one another, and they know me. They know that I cannot stand folding socks and that Diet Snapple Iced Tea is my favorite drink in the whole world. They also know that Stephanie is struggling because her grandpa has cancer, that Mike is excited because he got a new Labrador retriever puppy, that Lindsey got sixteen stitches after her forehead connected with the monkey bars in fourth grade, and that Nathan hasn't seen his dad in two years. My students learn that everyone has joy in his or her life and that everyone experiences pain. They know that they have a place where they can share their lives without fear of being teased. They know that their classmates will laugh with them, not at them.

They know that if they start to cry, they will be comforted. A case in point: one Monday morning, James shared that he'd had the worst weekend of his life because his dog had to be put down. Tears welled up in his eyes, and I thought, "Okay, this is a test of the degree of community in our classroom." I didn't have to wait long to see we'd passed. As James finished telling the story, an arm reached across the aisle and patted him on the back. Another student said, "Man, that's tough. I had to put my dog down last year, and I still cry about it." I couldn't have been more proud of my students as caring, compassionate beings. Moments like these are the moments when I silently say, "This is why I'm here. This is why I teach middle school."

From the outside, roll question looks easy. But as with almost everything, it's more complex than it seems. The foundation must be prepared— and the stronger the foundation, the more stable the structure.

Begin by explaining the purpose of roll question. Tell students that they are going to have to trust the people in our class, and the way to begin that relationship is to really know one another. Tell them that you want them to know you too, so you will always answer roll question yourself. The rules are simple:

» The time spent answering the roll question is sacred. Nothing goes on but listening to others and sharing when it is your turn. No reading a book or finishing your math or talking to a neighbor.

» If you don't wish to share, you can pass.

» There is a difference between laughing at someone and laughing with someone. (I have students explain what this means and give me an example.)

» Always tell the truth; don't feel you need to embellish your life to seem more exciting. We will love you just the way you are.

Sometimes I tell a story about why I've chosen the question—perhaps something that happened at home last night or something I've read in the newspaper. At the beginning of the year, the questions are low risk. As the kids get to know one another, the level of risk increases. Sometimes the questions are serious, but most times they are light and funny.

I describe this process as a ritual, because that's what it becomes. Heaven help me if, after the practice is established, I try to skip a day. I'm met with loud protests and an occasional (here it comes again!), "That's not fair!" Year after year, kids report that the roll question is what they most look forward to in their whole day. What I don't think they are able to vocalize is why. They say they love to hear others' stories and appreciate the way it allows them to ease into the class period, but I don't think they quite realize the impact of being in a place where they know and are known by others until they are older. There is security and comfort in a haven; that's what roll question creates.

On her own, a student wrote a "Where I'm From" poem about our class, in which she sweetly described her classmates and jokes and stories told. She finished the piece this way:

I come from a class where I feel I can be myself

without anyone caring what I'm wearing

or how I look

I'm from a loving seventh-grade writing class

Shouldn't every seventh grader feel this accepted and comfortable?

A list of potential roll questions appears in the appendix of this book. While you are more than welcome to use these questions, I urge you to tailor them to your students, the events in the world, and the issues you feel will make your classroom or school a better place.

In the best of relationships, neither party wants to disappoint the other. By helping kids know one another and allowing them to know us, we create a situation in which we all work a little harder for each other. Whenever I explain roll question, I always feel I haven't done it justice. A simple question, asked of thirty kids in a classroom, has the power to create a place kids want to be and a place I want to be. It also allows the sense of safety necessary for kids to be vulnerable and truly begin to write what is in their hearts and on their minds. As with anything new, it takes a while for roll question to become an established part of the day. Don't give up too soon; the potential is immeasurable.

Our world is full of systems that require certain conditions to thrive. Your classroom is no different. Who you are as a teacher and the environment you create has the power to impact your students in ways that inspire them to produce honest and meaningful texts. In creating that place in which you are consistent and predictable and your students are encouraged to accept and be accepted, you are giving kids so much more than writing instruction. You are making it okay simply to be. And in that security, the writing will blossom.

> **In creating that place in which you are consistent and predictable and your students are encouraged to accept and be accepted, you are giving kids so much more than writing instruction. You are making it okay simply to be.**

DIGGING DEEPER

Think of five words that describe your classroom. Ask yourself:

1. Which descriptors do I wish to keep and maintain as qualities of my classroom?

2. Which descriptors would I like to change? With what descriptors would I replace them?

3. How will I help my classes make this shift?

4. What will I need to see to know the change has occurred?

4

Cultivating Writing Practices

Increasing Writing Confidence by Giving Students What They Need

IF WE WANT OUR STUDENTS TO BE SKILLFUL, confident writers, we need to give them the necessary tools. We don't send people off to become electricians or astronauts by trial and error. We can't simply present "writerly" lessons and hope for the best. Our teaching must be intentional, our overarching goal to help students become better writers. They need meaningful instruction and opportunities to share their work with others.

Unique Considerations in Teaching Middle Schoolers

As teachers, we want our lessons to "stick." The ideas and skills we introduce to students are important, and we want them to remember and use the information when they write, now and in the future. For that to happen, lessons must be:

1. **Clear.** A lesson, whether on crafting titles or how to use a particular revision technique, should not leave students confused. By the end of instruction, they should thoroughly understand the information and be able to use it.

2. **Applicable.** Lessons taught when students need them have the best staying power. Avoid teaching lessons in isolation. A lesson on alliteration works better in a poetry unit than in a unit on research writing. Lessons presented when students can immediately apply the information or skill to their own work are especially effective.

3. **Transferable.** What students learn about writing should be used over time, in all kinds of writing situations. We want them to use revision techniques not only on their narrative writing but also on essays and fiction. Students sometimes compartmentalize what they learn, thinking that math happens only in math class and research happens only in science. Students should take what they learn in a writing class and instinctively apply it to composition in all subject areas.

As teachers of middle schoolers, we have an additional element to keep in mind: adolescent development. The kids in our classrooms have dynamic things happening to their brains and bodies. If lessons are to endure, we must take these conditions to heart. We need to:

> **The kids in our classrooms have dynamic things happening to their brains and bodies. If lessons are to endure, we must take these conditions to heart.**

1. **Maintain a singular focus.** Throwing too many concepts at middle schoolers ends in confusion. For some kids, that confusion is enough to make them check out. A lesson focused on a single skill or concept allows kids to settle down long enough to take in new information and internalize what is presented. Introducing too many ideas at once muddies the water. Keep lessons simple and uncluttered.

2. **Keep lessons short.** Middle school students have short attention spans. Don't give them time to check out; capture their attention, and deliver the information.

3. **Include opportunities to practice.** A chance to "do" strengthens the likelihood kids will hang on to new information. Don't stress theory at the expense of trying and applying. We remember what we do.

▌ The Minilesson

Quite possibly the most middle-school-friendly method of instruction is the minilesson. Minilessons are brief and purposeful and include time for practice. Middle schoolers and minilessons are a match made in heaven!

How are topics chosen?

While I'd like to tell you there is a giant book of minilessons that will turn your students into amazing writers, it's not true. The most notable quality of minilessons is that they allow you, the teacher, to use your experience, your observations, and your knowledge to identify what students need and decide how to get that information to them. Your experience tells you what skills students need to be able to write a memoir or a research paper successfully. You also see patterns in the skills students bring with them from their previous instruction. Use the knowledge you gather to present lessons that students need and will find useful.

Part of your life as a writing teacher is to develop and use your powers of observation. As you read students' drafts and confer with them about their writing problems, keep track of the skills and concepts that seem to be lacking. When several students make the same errors or when many students ask similar questions about practice, you know that a number of students have the same needs. These are excellent topics for minilessons.

We all have standards that guide our teaching. Because we are held accountable to these standards, students need to be proficient in the skills and concepts presented in them. However, the standards don't contain everything your students need to know. While you should be careful to include lessons that directly address the expectations of the standards, remember that minilessons about other useful writing topics are just as important.

> We all have standards that guide our teaching. Because we are held accountable to these standards, students need to be proficient in the skills and concepts presented in them. However, the standards don't contain everything your students need to know.

Your list of minilesson topics will be fluid. You may find that it's initially quite short. As you continue teaching, you'll observe student needs and develop minilessons that address them. Some years you may not use a particular minilesson because students already have the information or are not yet ready for it. The beauty of minilessons is that you use only what is applicable to the group in front of you. Why teach semicolons if your students are already using them correctly?

Here's a list of possible minilesson topics, in no particular order:

Steps in the Writing Process

What Is a Memoir?

Effective Introductions

Punctuating Dialogue

Run-On Sentences

I vs. *Me*

Good vs. *Well*

Verb Agreement

The Power of Strong Verbs

Wrapping It Up: Conclusions

Editing Marks

Prewriting Strategies

Drafting

Revision Strategies

Why Strive for Perfect in Final Drafts?

What to Think About for Your Final Draft

Headings and Formatting

Memoirs: Making Sure You've Covered All the Bases

Meter

To Rhyme or Not to Rhyme

The Blessing and the Curse: Rules and Poetry

How to Check Spelling If You Don't Know How to Spell a Word

Spell-Check Is Not Always Your Friend

Commas

Semicolons

Varying Sentence Length and Style

Where Writers Find Inspiration

Finding Writing Topics

The Rules of Story

Fiction: What to Do and What Not to Do

Crafting Good Titles

Examples and models

In the never-ending quest for clarity, we reinforce our instruction with examples of the types of writing we ask students to do and the practices we want them to use. A minilesson is the perfect venue for doing this.

History is full of people who have been inspired by the work of others. In the sciences, the work that happens today uses the knowledge and results obtained by yesterday's scientists. Painters learn technique by trying to reproduce the works of the masters. Writers and musicians inspired by other writers and musicians create new poems and songs.

Examples help us provide clear instruction. The work of others helps students answer the I'm-not-sure-what-to-do-here question by introducing more options and ideas. Each chapter in *Marley: A Dog Like No Other* (the middle school version of *Marley and Me*) by John Grogan provides an example of memoir as students construct their own. As students write poetry, *Love That Dog* by Sharon Creech demonstrates how to build a poem

> **Examples help us provide clear instruction.**

and how poetry is inspired by the things that matter most to us. Bringing in examples is also an opportunity to introduce students to the classics. A lesson on metaphor and simile is an excellent time to bring in the poetry and prose of William Shakespeare, to examine his writing as writers.

Minilessons in which we model performing a skill provide even more clarity for our students. It is one thing to present a carefully crafted lesson on a revision technique. We can talk about the benefits and outcomes of using the practice, but until they view it in action many students don't see it as real or useful. For example, to demonstrate the process of "cutting away" words that do not add to the beauty of a poem, put up a draft of one of your own poems. Tell students that when drafting poetry, many people write too much at first. Walk and talk them through the process of eliminating words to leave only those that best convey your message or image. Solicit their ideas too, to give kids a chance to try their hand at the revision strategy.

> **When students write, we tell them to "show, don't tell." Apply that same advice to your minilessons and see what happens!**

As middle school teachers, we know that immediate practice is very useful. After modeling, have students take their own drafts and practice the technique directly on their work. With the lesson fresh in their minds, the skill is more likely to stick with them and transfer to future writing. When students write, we tell them to "show, don't tell." Apply that same advice to your minilessons and see what happens!

A Sample Minilesson, From Planning to Implementation

Let's say you've noticed many of your students misusing (or not using!) commas. You decided to make proper comma use a minilesson.

» First, research the standards, including those for earlier grade levels, to identify which comma skills have (or should have) been taught. If you have noticed a hefty number of errors in all aspects of commas, you might reteach lessons from past grades.

» Tell students that one of the things you've noticed in their writing is some confusion around how to use commas. You might bring in Lynne Truss' *Eats, Shoots & Leaves* (the picture book version is wonderfully illustrated) to demonstrate how commas, though tiny marks, can change the meaning of sentences.

» Conduct a comma review, reminding students that this material was covered in their previous grades' writing lessons.

» Introduce standard comma practice at your grade level. If you have students keep a "writing handbook" (a notebook in which they record all writing minilessons throughout the year), have them copy the rule, including a properly punctuated example for future reference.

» Because immediate application is important, have students practice on five or six unpunctuated sentences. After students have added commas to a sentence, ask them how they know the commas are positioned correctly. Their version of the comma rule will either reinforce the correct punctuation they've provided or alert them that their punctuation is not correct and they need to amend their response.

» For additional practice, have students take out their current draft and read through it with the single intention of finding missing or incorrectly used commas. Circulate and confer, answering questions and helping students make corrections.

Remember, make your minilessons clear, applicable, transferable, focused, and short, with opportunities for practice. You'll be amazed by the power behind these simple but effective lessons.

And speaking of simple . . .

The term *academic rigor* is currently used with great frequency, and some may look at the concept of instruction through minilessons as too simple. I'll admit that when my students tell me they love my class because it is so easy, I feel a little unnerved. My job is to challenge and push students to grow. "Easy" sounds as if I'm not doing my job.

A conversation with a student shed some light on this dilemma. After he professed his love for my very easy class, I asked what he meant by *easy*. He told me that the work in class was not a cakewalk (he'd just finished his culminating project, sizeable by seventh-grade standards) but that "I always know what to do. That makes it easy."

Maybe our students associate *difficult* with *confusing* and *easy* with *clear*. Yes, an easy class could consist of fooling around, with nothing of merit accomplished. But the term might also be applied to rigorous but clear instruction. In the latter case, we've done a good job of fooling our students. They are working harder than ever (not seeming to realize it), producing great text, and they are happy to do so.

The writing requirements in the Common Core State Standards are easily addressed and practiced within the instructional model presented in this chapter. The ideas behind producing skilled and confident writ-ers are the same, no matter the standards. You do not need a purchased curriculum or some authority telling you what your writing students need. Those decisions, backed by the CCSS, are yours to make. After examining the expectations in the CCSS writing standards, you can create short, clear, and enduring lessons that will help students demonstrate these skills not only on writing tests but also—and more important—in all kinds of writing situations.

DIGGING DEEPER

Choose one of your writing assignments, and answer the following questions:

1. What writing skills do you know your students will need to complete this writing project successfully?
2. Which standards will be met if this project is completed successfully?
3. Is the purpose for your instruction clear? How will you draw students into the lessons and let them know how the information you present will benefit them?

> The why-are-we-learning-this lament is superseded when students understand that what we teach them is necessary for their growth as writers.

Clear, concise, meaningful minilessons lead to powerful learning because of their intent. The why-are-we-learning-this lament is superseded when students understand that what we teach them is necessary for their growth as writers. They gain information and confidence; so do we. By providing students with knowledge and skills that are useful and directly applicable, we enable our students to become the best writers they can be.

Opportunities to Communicate: Writing Groups, Conversations, and Open Mic

Think of all the reasons human beings talk—to connect, to create community, to entertain, to solve problems. We talk to console, to make our opinions known, to express our feelings. Talk binds us to one another; our words are as much for ourselves as for others.

Conversations around writing are no different. Writers talk about their work to share ideas, get feedback, solve problems, encourage others, and find common ground. When we talk, problems and possible solutions are clarified; we help one another. Our experiences are similar, so understanding runs deep.

While the act of writing is often solitary, part of our responsibility is to make sure students learn how to share their work with others. By participating in structured writing groups, having informal conversations about their writing, and going public with their words, students take the next important steps in their writing development.

> **While the act of writing is often solitary, part of our responsibility is to make sure students learn how to share their work with others.**

Writing groups

Writing groups have a number of purposes. First, they give students a chance to sit with a small group of peers and share their work in progress. Sharing what one has written can be frightening, especially in large groups. Being in a small group of three or four peers takes away a bit of that fear. Next, writing groups allow writers to get constructive feedback that boosts their confidence and points out sections of their text they might consider revising. Finally, writing groups teach kids how to listen with purpose and respond thoughtfully to others' writing.

Make writing groups work: an example. It would be nice if conducting writing groups were as simple as breaking middle school students into small groups and sending them on their way with, "Go talk together about your writing." They'd talk all right, but we couldn't guarantee the talk would be about students' current writing projects! It's middle school, where structure keeps kids on task and moving in the right direction.

There are many ways to design writing groups. Whatever the plan, the purpose should be the same: writers getting feedback on their work through the questions, ideas, and praise provided by group members. Here's one example.

Students arrive with their drafts, pencils, and response sheets (shown in Figure 4.1) for each author in the group. The group finds a place to sit so they are facing each other on the same level. When everyone is ready, they begin.

WRITING GROUP

Author's Name _____

Title/Working Title _____

Initial Impression (after first reading) _____

_____

_____

_____

_____

_____

_____

Wows	Wonders

Figure 4.1

Adapted with permission from the "Wows and Wonders" writing group response sheet
developed by the Puget Sound Writing Project, University of Washington, Seattle.

1. The first author introduces his writing. He might briefly share what inspired the piece, as well as ask for specific help. ("I'm having a tough time with the ending paragraph, so if you all could listen and offer suggestions, I'd appreciate it.")

2. The author reads his piece aloud; responders listen. When the author has finished reading, responders write their first reactions to the text.

3. As the author reads his piece aloud a second time, responders fill out the *Wows* and *Wonders* columns (wows for the elements of the piece that are impressive, wonders for the parts that may have been unclear, confusing, or out of place).

4. Responders share their feedback, one at a time, while the author takes notes directly on his draft. The author does not offer explanations for what he's written. He simply says thank you for the advice. This is not the time for the author to defend his intent; his purpose is gathering information to consider in his next round of revisions.

The group repeats this process with each successive author in the group.

Ideally, when the group session comes to a close, students go back to their drafts and consider the suggestions they've been given. Realizing that the responders have shared suggestions, they decide which changes they'll use to improve their work and which ones they'll ignore.

Teaching the process. Simply having a structure doesn't guarantee successful writing groups. Preteaching is necessary before students are sent off to their first writing group meeting. Since middle school students do better when they hear and see, modeling a writing group, with breaks for short commentary, gives kids a good idea of how they should perform when the time comes.

One way to provide this demonstration is to have your students gather in a circle with a writing group made up of teachers (or other adults you can enlist) at the center. Each adult brings a piece of writing, and together they conduct a writing group as students look on. The adults model giving feedback, making written responses, and being critical friends. Stop the demonstration from time to time for specific instruction: "Did you notice how Mrs. Williams told me that my third paragraph didn't seem strong enough? She didn't say, 'That third paragraph was horrible!' She stuck to the fact that it needed work without making me feel awful about it."

Teaching students how to provide feedback is essential. The goal of a writing group is to make everyone's writing better. While statements such as "I like it" or "That was fantastic!" might make an author feel good, they do not offer opportunities for positive changes. Having students practice writing helpful feedback, rather than judgments, is one more way to ensure successful writing group experiences.

What if writing groups don't go smoothly? Part of our job is to monitor and adjust. A writing group plan that looks great on paper may not go so well when you add the variable: middle school kids. Remember that this kind of peer-to-peer communication may be very new for your students. They are also operating independently: you cannot monitor all the groups at the same time. Groups might encounter an uncooperative member or someone who expresses discomfort by acting out and derailing progress. There is nothing wrong with tweaking the process to make it better. Perhaps you'll add a new element to each writing group meeting to keep kids on their toes. Maybe you'll keep the same groups all year long, or maybe you'll reconfigure them with each project. The important thing is to keep kids talking about their own work and the work of their peers. Part of the writing process is the journey, and writing groups play an enriching role in producing meaningful text.

> **The important thing is to keep kids talking about their own work and the work of their peers.**

Informal conversations

Not all learning activity in classrooms has to be engineered and monitored. Getting students to talk to one another about writing can produce ideas, solutions to problems, and camaraderie, with relatively no planning or prepwork on your part. Some conversations can be held with the entire class, some between a few students or one-on-one. Some take place without your even knowing it!

Large-group conversations. The craft of writing overflows with topics for whole-class conversation. Writers are free to use their creativity, and form, structure, word choice, and imagery lend themselves to all kinds of interesting conversations. "Metaphors," a poem by Sylvia Plath, prompts students to discuss why the number nine keeps showing up and its importance to the poem. Students can consider why John Grogan refers to Marley's tail as his "wildly wagging weapon." Open-ended conversations like these get kids thinking and offering ideas, using the thoughts and opinions of others as springboards. When you hear students say, "I agree with what Nate said, but what if . . . ," you know kids are listening to one another and integrating the ideas of others into their own thoughts.

> When you hear students say, "I agree with what Nate said, but what if . . . ," you know kids are listening to one another and integrating the ideas of others into their own thoughts.

Small-group conversations. Small-group conversations are a little more intimate, so consider saving higher-risk topics for these situations. For example, at the end of a writing session, say, "Turn to a neighbor, and share the best line or two that you wrote today." Or ask a row or table of students to gather and share opinions on the most difficult aspect of editing, each person explaining why. Smaller groups can also have conversations about favorite words, authors they admire, and why revision is such an important part of writing. These conversations may stray from the original topic; the important thing is to get kids talking to one another and sharing their views on writing.

One-on-one conferences during class. The term *writing conference* covers a span of possibilities. A conference is a teacher and a student talking about writing. Some conferences are structured and formal; others are more informal and based on a student's immediate need or struggle. While your students are writing, stop by their desks and get kids to talk. Asking, "How are things going?" or "What has been difficult about writing this piece?" or "Would you read a few lines to me so I can get the flavor of your story?" solicits information for planning future instruction, gives you insight into students' development, and gives your students a chance to verbalize successes and stumbling blocks.

Conversations that may or may not involve you. The conversations that surprise and delight me most are the ones taking place without my knowledge. I love finding out that two kids have rushed through their lunches so they can meet in the library and edit each other's paper. Or overhearing,

"Hey, don't forget your draft so we can help each other with revisions on the bus ride home." Or having a kid tell me, "Andy came over to my house so we could help each other with our poems." Also be alert to the conversations kids initiate with you between classes or on the way to lunch. Some of the best insights I've gained about kids and writing have come from unexpected talks I've had with them in the halls or while waiting for the buses to arrive. Just because they are unplanned and informal doesn't make them less important or less valuable. Because they spring from very real needs, they are, perhaps, the most genuine conversations of all!

Open mic

The most important and possibly scariest aspect of sharing words is standing up before a group and reading what one has written. Mention this possibility, and many middle schoolers will back away, saying, "No, no, no, no, no. Please don't make me."

Open mic in the classroom mimics what happens in coffeehouses, theaters, libraries, and all kinds of venues. Individuals sign up to share their work for the experience of providing enjoyment to others. It can take place during the school day or be an evening event to which parents and other guests are invited.

To hold an open mic, you'll need a room big enough for an audience. Having a microphone helps all audience members hear and gives readers the experience of speaking into one. A podium gives nervous readers a place to rest their papers and (if they're feeling really jittery) something to hold on to. Before you begin, make it very clear that the people getting up to read are brave souls who deserve nothing less than full attention from audience members. Those listening are responsible for appropriate audience behavior. One by one, volunteers read, often making their peers laugh at the funny pieces or sit in attentive silence in response to those that are emotional. Some students who initially balked at reading their work will see how safe this forum is, so always ask whether anyone else wishes to share after everyone on the list of signed-up volunteers has been heard.

I wish I could adequately convey what reading at an open mic does for young writers. The respect they get from their peers and that rush of doing something that scares them makes kids take extra pride in their work. I love hearing the conversations as we walk back to class. The readers always seem to walk a little taller after their classmates tell them how much they enjoyed hearing their work.

Additional ways to share

Taking words to a larger audience can happen in other ways too. During morning announcements in April—National Poetry Month—have students read poems they've written. Publish pieces in your school's monthly newsletter. Watch for open mics or competitions in your community. Ask a local author or two to come in and listen to the work of small groups of writers. Whatever the venue, helping kids share what they've crafted is an important step we simply cannot miss.

DIGGING DEEPER

1. In your next unit of study, what questions can you generate that will prompt large-group conversations? Small-group conversations?
2. What opportunities for sharing students' writing already exist in your school or community?
3. What can you create that allows students the opportunity to take their words to others?

Trust Yourself: You Know More Than You Think You Know!

Being confident in your practice is difficult when you try something new. The best learning and growing will take place when you trust yourself and the knowledge you have. Stay in tune with your students and where they are in their writing development so you'll know where to begin planning the lessons that create success. Trust your instincts as you reflect on learning and conversations around writing. Know that you'll get better at this over time. Your confidence in what you see and hear is the catalyst for the very best writing your students can produce.

5

Responding Authentically

Evaluating Student Writing

ASK ANY TEACHER about evaluating student writing and you'll get two predictable responses: it takes a lot of time and it's difficult. We all went into teaching language arts knowing that we weren't in a discipline that could grade most work in class, so the long hours for evaluation are nothing new. And there's no doubt the task is difficult. Writing involves fewer right-or-wrong answers. Any given topic can produce thirty different views in any given class, none more correct than the others. In the past, we've chosen to deal with the aspects of writing that are more easily measured, like conventions. Teachers have also provided well-meaning but vague comments in margins like "good idea," "develop this," and my personal favorite, "nice." What, exactly, does *nice* mean in terms of writing?

▌Young Writers Need Feedback

Feedback, by definition, is an evaluative response. Our students need honest feedback that builds confidence, points out places to improve, and provides inspiration and encouragement to continue working toward better writing.

Feedback that builds confidence

Students often categorize themselves as one of two kinds of writer: good or bad. They fail to recognize that all good writing has the potential for weak points and that it is possible for some pretty awful writing to have some redeeming value. Through feedback, we are able to point out those aspects of students' writing that are working well.

Sometimes students may not have written anything particularly brilliant, but we still point out "a good technique" or "a clever arrangement of words" to let them know they've written something of worth. I'm not saying we should manufacture praise. Kids can spot phony accolades a mile away and what they perceive as fake acknowledgment might diminish your authority in their eyes. Work to keep your responses genuine.

> Students often categorize themselves as one of two kinds of writer: good or bad. They fail to recognize that all good writing has the potential for weak points and that it is possible for some pretty awful writing to have some redeeming value.

Feedback that points out places to improve

While it's great to hear positive praise of our work, building greater writing confidence does not single-handedly make better writers. If the purpose of evaluation is to improve students' writing skills, feedback should also indicate areas in students' work that need more attention. In addition to finding out what works well within a piece, students also need to know where things break down. As an evaluator, you might point out places in the writing that could use more clarity or detail. You might note that the title doesn't quite fit the piece or that there are too many misspelled words for a final draft. These comments are never threatening or judgmental. Your honest and helpful feedback is meant to make your students better writers. Once they trust that you are working with them to achieve that goal, they'll understand and take seriously the thoughts you pass along.

> Building greater writing confidence does not single-handedly make better writers.

Feedback that encourages and inspires students to move forward

A child's response to feedback should never be dismay and complete despair. No matter how dismal the writing, your feedback needs to identify the redeeming qualities. Students should always walk away knowing that what they've written is not a complete loss. They should understand that there are ways to improve, that you are willing to help them in any way necessary, and that you have complete faith in their abilities as writers. All children can write, no matter their skill levels, gifts, or difficulties. Your feedback has an enormous impact on the progress your students make as writers. Your message of "you can do this and here's how" might be the difference between a student deciding to try again or disposing of her work in the nearest recycle bin.

> No matter how dismal the writing, your feedback needs to identify the redeeming qualities. Students should always walk away knowing that what they've written is not a complete loss.

A word about how students respond to feedback

Don't be surprised if students have mixed reactions to your honest and specific feedback. For some kids, this may be the first time someone has carefully scrutinized their work. Some students may be shocked at how well they've done on a piece, especially if they are convinced they are "bad" writers. Those who've spent their lives hearing only positive things about their writing may be alarmed by suggestions for improvement. Neither situation should deter you from providing feedback designed to make better writers. The kids used to getting low grades for their work will eventually understand that they have great writing potential. It may take them a while to believe you, but they'll get there, especially as you balance honest praise with the acknowledgment of areas needing more consideration. Students not accustomed to anything less than an A or to someone pointing out areas that need improvement may be a little off balance with you for a while, but they, too, will come around.

I have frank and honest conversations with my students about the feedback they'll get from me. Before they read the evaluations on their first project, we talk about how my job is to make them better writers, no matter their writing skills when they walked through my door. I tell them I'll be unfailingly honest and if something isn't working, I'll let them know. On the other hand, if I believe they've done something particularly clever or skillful, I'll praise them. We talk about how my feedback is not personal and that what I say is not a reflection on them; it is a reflection on one piece of their writing.

> **My feedback is not personal and what I say is not a reflection on them; it is a reflection on one piece of their writing.**

Does this change students' expectations and reactions regarding my evaluations? Not at first, but as we progress through the year, students begin to depend on that honest reaction to their work. Even those who initially wished you'd do nothing but gush about their writing eventually take solid, honest evaluation over meaningless praise any day.

The Great Divide: Separating the Writing from Writing Behavior

> **How we share our thoughts with students can either build them up and encourage them to move forward or shut them down, making them less likely to revisit their writing to make improvements.**

Teachers spend all day giving advice. Informally, we offer our opinions on students' work while they are in the formative stages of creating and constructing. When they've finished, we offer more summative feedback. How we share our thoughts with students can either build them up and encourage them to move forward or shut them down, making them less likely to revisit their writing to make improvements. There are many methods for letting students know how they've done. In this chapter I'll share three feedback tools that work together to present balanced and comprehensive evaluations: a writing behavior rubric, a genre rubric, and narrative feedback.

Before we tackle these tools, though, consider an attitude adjustment regarding your beliefs about evaluation. Admit it: there are things kids do in class that drive us crazy. I'm not talking about whispering or texting or falling asleep. I'm talking about academic behavior outside the bounds of what we think kids should do:

» Sitting in class, apparently indifferent, never seeming to pay attention, but turning in assignments that clearly show they were not only listening but applying what we taught to their work!

» Listening and always participating in class but when it's time to turn in an assignment, they never have it. It's been lost or, better yet, *stolen*.

» Working on writing projects in class but never having the work done when it's due.

» Turning in final drafts with no name or in a condition that suggests the paper was folded up, stuffed in a pocket, and sent through the laundry.

» Not doing the assignments we've designed to help students become better writers, then turning in an outstanding final draft. (How *dare* they!)

Our job, as writing teachers, is to produce better writers. Writing is a product of our students' efforts, something that can stand alone and be evaluated, in whatever manner it was produced. While the behavior illustrated in the list above might cause us great frustration, it is separate from a finished piece of writing. It has nothing to do with organization, content, voice, conventions, message, and author's purpose; it has to do with choices and decisions students make, like it or not.

The bottom line is that we, as teachers, cannot always control the decisions students make in relation to their writing; we can, however, control how the writing is evaluated. Therefore, we need to separate the writing from writing behavior. We can still grumble about "not following the rules" and grade these behavioral choices. Then we need to put that aspect of evaluation aside and look at the students' work for what it is: writing. We don't have to say to ourselves, "This is fantastic writing, but darn it! He turned it in late! Again!" Our energy can now be directed to providing honest and helpful feedback on the writing itself.

The writing behavior rubric

This rubric addresses the behaviors you want students to exhibit during all their writing experiences—the things to keep in mind in relation to their memoirs, their poetry, their research papers, any kind of writing they do, now and in the future. This rubric remains constant all year long applied to all final drafts turned in for evaluation. An example is provided in Figure 5.1. You decide the weight you give this rubric in the overall evaluation—for information only or part of the overall grade. Whichever you choose, remember that the purpose of the rubric is to allow you to put the rules aside and simply focus on evaluating the writing.

Figure 5.1 Writing Behavior Rubric

	Excellent (2 points)	Satisfactory (1 point)	Needs Work (0 points)
Met the Deadline	The piece was turned in on time.	(Not applicable.)	The piece was not turned in on time.
History	Detailed writing history (brainstorming, prewriting, drafts) was turned in with the piece.	An acceptable amount of history was turned in with the piece.	Little, if any, history was turned in with the piece.
Correct Format for Genre	The piece is in the correct format and follows the guidelines for the genre.	The piece is close to the correct format but may have strayed from some of the guidelines for the genre.	The piece is not in the correct format for the genre.
Presentation	The piece is typed or written in blue/black ink and is double spaced if required. Supporting papers are neatly arranged in order. Final drafts are flat and clean. It's obvious the author took pride in his/her work.	The piece is typed or written in blue/black ink. Supporting papers are mostly in order. Final drafts are mostly flat and clean. The author could have taken a bit more pride in turning in neat work.	The piece is not typed or written in ink. Final drafts are wrinkled and/or dirty. The piece was hastily put together and/or does not reflect pride in the author's work.
Heading and Title	The piece has an appropriate heading (full name, period, date) and a carefully crafted title.	The piece has an appropriate heading but may be missing a minor element or two. The title is present.	The piece has an incomplete heading (missing name) and/or is missing a title.

(Developed by Kathy Williams and Shelley Barker, Centennial Middle School, Snohomish, Washington.)

The genre rubric

This rubric changes with the type of writing. The criteria in the left column should reflect the content and lessons you taught during the unit, as well as any overall criteria you wish to include. An example of a memoir rubric is provided in Figure 5.2.

Rubrics are most useful when student writers understand how they'll be used as evaluative tools. Give both rubrics to students at the beginning of a writing project. Teach them how to use the rubrics before, during, and after the writing process to answer some of the questions they have while drafting the piece and preparing to hand in their final draft.

Narrative Feedback: A Chance to Personalize Response

> Rubrics are effective because they give students clear targets before, during, and after they write. However, rubrics don't express all we'd like to share with students.

Rubrics are effective because they give students clear targets before, during, and after they write. However, rubrics don't express all we'd like to share with students. Ideally, we'd be able to sit down with students one-on-one and talk for ten or fifteen minutes, telling them what we've noticed specifically about their writing. However, because of large class sizes, I've not found a time-efficient way to conduct face-to-face conferences; therefore, I provide narrative feedback instead.

The structure of narrative feedback

My narrative feedback takes the form of a letter to the writer. I begin with my general impression of the piece or the way I connected with the student's writing. I then provide a running commentary of what I see going well within the piece. Here, I can be specific about what the writer has done to make this piece effective. The next section comments on places in the piece that are weak and need more attention. Again, I can be specific in describing the problem and suggesting possible solutions. I conclude with some sort of encouragement: congratulating the writer on a job

Figure 5.2 Memoir Rubric

	Outstanding (4 points)	Standard (3 points)	Emerging (2 points)	Not Evident (1 point)
Lead	The lead prompts questions and interest; it grabs the reader's attention and pulls him/her into the writing. The reader feels compelled to stay and read.	The lead is interesting and gets the reader's attention.	The lead is present but does not prompt questions or interest.	The lead is not present.
Topic	The topic is narrow. The author focuses on an important sliver of time and works to "dig deep" rather than cover too much ground.	The topic is mostly narrow, but sometimes the author attempts to cover too much ground.	The topic is broad with few examples of deep description.	The writing is a list of events.
Purpose	Topic importance can easily be identified by the reader. It is subtle or implied.	Topic importance can be identified by the reader.	Potential for identifying importance is present but not fully developed.	No topic importance is discernible.
Showing vs. Telling	The author brings the reader along for the ride. Descriptions show rather than tell. The reader feels like he/she is right there in the moment.	The author uses descriptions that mostly show rather than tell. The reader is mostly engaged in the moment.	The author uses descriptions that mostly tell rather than show. There are some instances of bringing the reader along for the ride.	The author uses descriptions that tell rather than show.
Conclusion	The conclusion brings the piece to a natural close that is connected to the topic. It does not include "And that is why" or "The End" as a way to finish.	The conclusion brings the piece to a close. It does not include "And that is why" or "The End" as a way to finish.	The conclusion is attempted but is awkward or disconnected from the topic. It may include "And that is why" or "The End" as a way to finish.	No conclusion is present.
Strong Verbs	The author consistently uses strong verbs to enhance writing.	The author mostly uses strong verbs.	The author uses some strong verbs, but many verb choices weaken the writing.	The author rarely uses strong verbs.
Conventions (includes dialogue formatting)	The piece contains very few spelling or grammar errors in the piece.	The piece contains some spelling and grammar errors in the piece.	More time could have been spent editing spelling and grammar errors.	The piece contains major spelling and grammar errors.

(Developed by Kathy Williams and Shelley Barker, Centennial Middle School, Snohomish, Washington.)

well done or inspiring her or him to rewrite the draft on the basis of the advice given on the rubrics and in my letter. I end by signing my name. This keeps the feedback personal, reminding students that the advice is coming from me: the person who knows they can be successful and effective writers.

An example of narrative feedback on work that meets expectations

Gracie started seventh grade as a strong writer and continued to make good progress as her writing confidence and skill level rose. In December she wrote the following poem and turned it in for evaluation.

X-Ray of Me

I've changed this year,
Not completely for the better.
I used to have straight A's,
What's happened to my school work?

Some call me mean
Some call me kind.
I don't mean to be mean,
I'm trying to be kind.

I miss my mom
And my dad,
The relationship
From the past.
Does being a teenager
Mean disrespecting your parents?

Some things have improved,
I'm social now.
Last year wasn't fun,
Now I can rely on friends.

I've don't get in trouble.
Never again.

If only there was an x-ray machine
For personalities.

My narrative feedback to Gracie is shown below. It acknowledges what is working well, points out the places where she might make revisions, and encourages her to keep making positive growth in her writing.

Gracie A.
Free-Verse Poem
December 9, 2011

Gracie, you'll be pleased to know that you are not the only teenager going through the turmoil you present in this poem. It's nice to know you are not alone, right?

I'm pleased to see you chose a topic that means something to you. Your unsettled feelings about these changes feel very real to your readers (especially those who have already gone through adolescence) because you are so honest in what you write. You step up and own lower grades, being perceived as mean, and the changes in the relationship with your parents. When I first glanced at your second stanza, I was worried when I saw the word mean *three times, in such close proximity. You made it work, though! Nothing felt redundant in that stanza; in fact, it came across as quite clever. Good technique.*

We discussed in class that how a poem looks on paper is important. Your first, second, and fourth stanzas were uniform in numbers of lines. I'm wondering why you chose to make the third stanza longer. The last two are different as well. I'd love to know more. There are a few places you might consider showing rather than telling. Specifically, I'm thinking of the line, "I'm social now." Is there a way you can prove that rather than simply stating it?

I believe there is a word mix-up in the first line of your fifth stanza. Can you clear that up and show it to me later? I can see a couple of possibilities, but I don't want to guess.

My favorite part of this poem is the last two-line stanza. It seems as if you just want to know you are okay as a person and wish you could find out in the same way we use x-ray machines to look at things we can't readily see. Love that connection! Good writing.

I'm pleased with the writing progress you continue to make. You are a strong writer who keeps getting stronger through your dedication and hard work! Keep writing!

Mrs. B.

An example of narrative feedback on work that doesn't meet expectations

Jacob had a negative past when it came to writing. His work in previous grades was "never good enough," he reported, so his opinion of his writing ability was quite low when he entered seventh grade. This memoir was his first piece.

(No Title)

I am writing about my dog tabby when we got her she was a sweet little tiny puppy my dad could fit her in his hand. She had puppy breath which I thought was bad then but smell her breath now and you'll miss the puppy breath. One good thing about her getting older is her teeth got duller instead of little dagers she was scared of every thing max did max is my other dog but she will fight him every chance she gets now. she gets very jelous when we pet max so we have to hide when we pet max. Most of what we think of her is a big dork having random spaz attacks.

My feedback for Jacob (see next) strikes a careful balance between pointing out changes that need to be made (there are many!) and providing the encouragement to try again. I word this feedback in a way that doesn't overwhelm him yet still lets him know how to proceed.

Jacob B.
Narrative Writing
October 1, 2011

I may be biased, but dogs make the very best pets. I have really enjoyed the Tabby stories you've told in class and I'm glad you made her the topic of your memoir.

I'm impressed by how strong your voice is in this piece. The lines you wrote about not liking Tabby's puppy breath but then realizing it was better than her grown-up dog breath sounded just like something you'd say in a conversation. Your word choice is strong too, especially when you compared those sharp puppy teeth to daggers. Anyone who has raised a puppy will relate to that!

Remember that the purpose of an introduction is to invite your reader to stay and read your story. Your first line certainly makes a clear beginning, but I'm wondering if there is a more enticing way to start this piece. In class we talked about starting with a story. Is there a tale you could use to create instant interest for your reader?

Since you talk about Tabby being so small she'd fit in your dad's hand, maybe you could use the story of going to pick her up. Do you think that would work?

And while we're talking about stories, do you think there are a few more you could include to add more interest? Remember how we talked in class about showing rather than telling? Maybe a story about the damage those sharp little puppy teeth did or how she goes to battle with Max? Those extra details give your reader the gift of a complete story.

I'm thinking you just forgot to craft a title for this piece. Don't forget to add one!

You are missing a lot of punctuation. I'd like you to sit down in a quiet place with your memoir and a pencil. Read your work out loud and add punctuation where you think it should go. You'll catch most of your errors! Remember that names are always capitalized. You have a few spelling errors, but I think you'll catch them as you read through again. If not, see me.

I hope you'll rework this piece and turn it in to me again. This story has the potential to be really good, and you have all the potential in the world to become an even better writer! Keep writing!

Mrs. B.

Let's get real: narrative feedback seems like a lot of work!

No argument here. It *is* a lot of work. Rubrics can be quick, but narrative feedback takes time and energy. Before you dismiss it on the grounds that your life is crazy enough as is, consider the following:

1. **Daily grading is diminished (and maybe disappears completely!).** You are evaluating a final draft, one that took several weeks to produce. Students have turned in the history of the project with the piece, so you are not grading every aspect of their writing along the way. You might go weeks without evaluating and recording grades.

2. **Projects replace tests.** Students show you what they can do by producing text. This eliminates the need for quizzes and tests; all the proof you need is in what students write and the feedback you give them.

3. **You'll give less feedback over time.** At first, students need that contact with you. They need to know they are doing some things well and that others need revision. One of your goals over time should be to make students more independent writers. This includes leading

them to rely more on themselves for evaluation. As the year progresses, have students evaluate themselves on the rubrics before they turn in work. Later, limit your responses to three to five short comments regarding big changes.

4. **This kind of feedback has a big impact.** My students tell me they benefit from "the letters," as they call them. ("Your letters always tell me what I need to think about and how to get there.") My students know I've taken time to focus on their work, and they take my advice seriously. That alone keeps me going on late nights and on long grading weekends.

If Writing Is a Process, Shouldn't We Get to Try Again?

Traditionally, turning in work is the end of the line. Work comes in, we attach a grade and return it to the students, the class moves on to the next topic. However, when we stop mixing writing and writing behavior—when the writing becomes most important—a new possibility emerges:

1. We must recognize that writing can always be improved.
2. We must recognize that the feedback we provide is designed to make students' writing better.
3. If (2) is true, a final draft really isn't "final."

Allow students another opportunity to be successful.

> **What would happen if you allowed all your students to try again on any writing project they complete for your class?**

If we truly stand behind our mission to create confident and skillful writers, we have to instill the processes that allow this to happen. At the same time, we can help students view their progress as an opportunity to become better writers rather than base their sense of success on grades.

What would happen if you allowed all your students to try again on any writing project they complete for your class? What if you said, "If you are not happy with the results of your work, look at the feedback and give it another try"? Take it a step further by letting students know that there will be no grade penalty for trying again. If the reworked writing is reevaluated as A work, the new grade is an A, not an average of the original grade and the new grade. What would this opportunity do for your students?

There are benefits of a second (or third or fifth) chance.

The game changes when students know they'll have a chance to revise their work with no penalty for trying again:

1. **Another chance gives validity to the writing process.** If we preach that writing is a process but give only one chance to get it right, we're contradicting ourselves.

2. **Another chance = less stress = more risks.** When students realize their evaluation isn't tied to one attempt, they allow themselves to get away from "getting it right" and venture into more creative ways to express themselves. Does that exploration always create success? Of course not, but no one grows by keeping things safe.

3. **Another chance allows students more practice.** Can you think of any process where one learns something and demonstrates mastery in one shot? We allow (in fact, we demand!) surgeons to practice on cadavers before they do the real thing! Another chance means more practice for our writers, which simply makes them better.

4. **Another chance creates ownership.** When a student deliberately decides to make improvements to something he's written, he's taken ownership. The writing belongs to him, and he's doing everything in his power make it good because the writing *is* him; the two cannot be separated.

But what if . . . ?

The skeptic in all of us comes out when we are faced with a new idea. What happens to the work ethic when students are allowed to try again? Will kids slack off and not produce their best effort the first time because they know they'll have another shot? How will kids view deadlines and responsibility if the process is open to more revision?

The chance to try again does not create less work—if anything, it creates more! A student who doesn't do her best work, intending to revise later, doesn't get out of anything. She's now doing double time, keeping up with current work and the work she neglected before. Same for the kids who slack off and turn in work that is incomplete. They didn't get a free pass! Those who struggle with deadlines have probably struggled all along and will continue to struggle until they see a need to be prompt.

Kids who try to game the system do so to get out of work. Once they figure out they've created more work for themselves, they get smart. To be honest, very few of my students have tried to take unfair advantage of the opportunity to try again. I feel safe saying the opposite is true. Kids see this chance as a way to take charge of their work. It becomes a privilege, not an exercise in avoiding work.

At the beginning of this chapter, you read that responding to students' writing is time consuming and difficult. It is still time consuming and difficult, but I hope you are now able to see beyond those two descriptors. It is through our careful efforts in responding to students' writing that they make tremendous growth. What we point out, both in praise and with the intent to improve, makes a difference in the writing skills and the confidence levels of our students. From our words, kids learn how to become writers. Our efforts beget their efforts, and that is beautifully satisfying!

6

Celebrating Increased Student Skill and Confidence

PERHAPS THE BIGGEST CONFIDENCE BUILDERS, both for teachers and students, are the results, the work that is produced by student writers who have been surrounded by choice, meaningful instruction, encouragement, and honest feedback. We recognize the moments of success by observing, so watch for these possibilities to arise in your writing classroom:

1. **Kids are comfortable with all kinds of writing tasks.** Don't be surprised when you find students becoming more at ease with the act of writing. Teachers make all kinds of assumptions about their students' abilities to write. Our past lessons may have been more "just write" than "here's how to write." Kids who have been taught how to write report that they finally know what to do when it comes to composition. Instead of being turned loose, down lots of confusing paths that take them to unknown destinations, they know where to begin, where to end, and what to include in the middle. "Writing is no longer this big confusing mess," one of my students wrote in a midyear evaluation. We have the ability to see to it that all our students can make that claim!

2. **Kids mix things up a bit.** Watch for students who become more willing to take risks and be creative. With permission to try again, you'll

> **Don't be surprised when you find students becoming more at ease with the act of writing.**

see students step out of the box and allow themselves to be daring and clever. One year, a student turned in a final draft that was crumpled in a ball. I make a big deal out of pristine final drafts. Final work should show a sense of pride, right? As I began to protest the wad of paper before me, the girl said, "Please. Let me explain." She went on to share that the piece was inspired by her anger at her biological dad, who left shortly after she'd been born and never made an effort to be in her life. What stung even more was the fact he lived two towns away and had started a new family, leaving my student feeling even more abandoned. She wanted to show her anger in a way without words to really get her meaning across. Mission accomplished!

3. **Kids see themselves as writers.** Realize that students will begin to see writing as a legitimate outlet. Don't be surprised when kids start telling you and showing you that writing has become more than something they do for a grade at school. You might start to hear questions like, "How old do you have to be to publish a book?" which can lead to wonderful conversations about how writing knows no age limits and that very young people have successfully published in all kinds of formats. Students might slip a poem or two your way, even after they've moved up a grade level (or five). They'll ask you to read a speech they've written to campaign for a class office or accept an award. They'll proudly announce that they've started a novel, wave a comp book in front of your face, and say, "And I've already written fifteen pages." All of this writing is taking place outside your realm! They recognize you as a writing ally and a writing authority. They write because they know how and why; you can be very proud to be a part of that!

> **Don't be surprised when kids start telling you and showing you that writing has become more than something they do for a grade at school.**

4. **Kids use the writing process as naturally as a cell phone or a toothbrush.** Mark the moments when students begin to use all the steps

of the writing process, willingly, on their own, and without complaint! These are indications that writing practices are taking root in students' lives. For example, at the beginning of a writing project, you may be talking with students about possible ideas. When you give them some time to think and plan, out come papers and pencils, and all kinds of prewriting organizers are sketched. Or when students complete their very first draft of a piece, they take out the pens or colored pencils and begin revising without your reminder (or demand!). My heart always jumps a little when this happens, and a voice in my head whispers, "They're doing it! They're using the writing process on their own!" Each step means something because you've taught it, demonstrated it, and proven that writing is better when it's been through a complete and thoughtful process.

Examples of Writing by Skilled and Confident Writers

Another of the many joys in my job is reading some pretty incredible work written by students. The five pieces below are just a smattering of what I read in a year. All are products of writing projects in my seventh-grade classes. None of the students were told what to write; each was responsible for searching his or her own brain for a topic of importance and then conveying it in the best way he or she knew how. Nothing was forced or directed by me or anyone else; the path each piece took and the subsequent finished product were wrought by the hands of twelve- and thirteen-year-olds.

A poem by Maryanne Proffit

Maryanne is bright and funny. She thinks deeply, asks thoughtful questions, and is excellent at finding the nuances in everyday events. She wrote "The Girl on the Page" in response to two sources: a print advertisement for cosmetics and the Dove Real Beauty campaign video. The print ad consisted of a flawless, attractive face. The video used time-lapse photography to show a fashion model's transformation from the moment she walked into the studio, through her hair and makeup session, and finally to the computer-aided editing that made her eyebrows perfect, neck longer, and skin blemish-free. The question of "What is real?" and the issues surrounding physical perfection were her inspiration for this poem.

The Girl on the Page

As I sit in the chair
I see my face staring back at me with no expression
I hear opinions about what to change, what is not right
I feel the layer of makeup on my skin, making me feel fake and ugly underneath.

As I stare into the camera lens
I see my reflection and my solemn face
I hear the photographer telling me how to pose
I feel the thought in the back of my mind, reminding me that computers will
            change me into a whole new person.

As I sit on the bench
I see a face on the page that I almost do not recognize
I hear the photographers' voices echo in my head
I feel my self esteem drop.

As I stand up
I see my hands tremble as they move down the page
I hear the sound of girls wanting look at the girl on the page
I feel the need to be my own person, not something someone makes me.

I see the ripped pages fluttering in the wind.

Besides triggering conversations about good poetry techniques (repetition, balance, and word choice), a poem like Maryanne's gives a unique view into a student's developing sense of self. We are so lucky to be able to get to know our students so well!

A narrative by Anthony Ray

Anthony is at ease with language. Though his preferential topics center more on fantasy and sci-fi (with a little video-game-ese thrown in for fun!), he wrote this short piece about moving from the home he'd always known to where he lives now. There is a certain sweet sadness in the writing, as he describes the last walk through his house.

Redmond

I walk through the halls one last time. My mom calls, "Come on, it's time to go." As I go through the door, I remember everything about this house. I'll never see it again, my entire life so far, just taken and whisked about to a small rural town called Snohomish. The house feels empty and sad.

As I walk into my old bedroom, I remember staying up late into the night playing Xbox, hoping my mom wouldn't catch me. I remember waking up at three in the morning, crawling in bed with my brothers because I'd had a nightmare. Now, I'll just have to stay up at night, hoping the clutches of sleep don't bring me into another horrible world.

I enter the living room and notice the place where our frog, that ran away, used to live. I remember holding him and only thinking about how slimy he was. What I would give to hold him again. I remember waking up to gentle shaking at midnight, Stephen's leading Gregory and me into the living room to watch the shows Mom forbade.

Stepping into our backyard brings another wave of memories. I step to the spot where our dead hamster, Anakin, now lays in eternal sleep. I step into the middle of the lawn and remember the forty to fifty mile per hour winds that hit my body with such force that I was blown back. Then, stepping inside, still freezing because the power was out. It felt warmer when I snuggled up to my mom and fell asleep. Now the yard was going to be someone else's. I wonder what they'd say if they found Anakin.

I step out the door one final time and start a new life in a new house. Sometimes I still wonder about that little apartment and wonder who the new owners are. That apartment will always be my house.

Anthony's farewell to his home marks his growing understanding that things change and that even if changes are good, they are still a little sad. The room-by-room tour is a good example of writing that takes the reader "along for the ride."

A poem by Adair Trachta-Magruder

Adair entered seventh grade with a knack for writing fiction better than many adults. Adair's family had just moved from Texas to Washington, and this poem encapsulates her first encounter with a substantial snowfall.

Nighttime Snow

Amber lights
Bounce around.
They create
A glowing ground.
Pearly earth;
A plain white sheet.
This is where
Land and clouds meet.
Amethyst clouds
Block silver light
And branches reach
Into purple night.
Emerald branches
On evergreen trees
Make not a sound
In the nighttime breeze
The world is still;
Nothing but silence,
And in this moment,
There is no violence
Take in the beauty
Of this frozen land,
Catch the falling diamonds
In my cold hand.
I write down this moment
So that all the world will know
Of the crystalline world
Of the nighttime snow.

Adair's poem is a manifestation of writing about a moment in time and keeping a narrow focus. The skills kids learn as poets strengthen their other writing as well. Make sure your students know that their poetry skills will help them write clearly and succinctly in prose too.

A narrative piece by Jess Harris

Jess is a writer who composes text that sounds just like a conversation with him. Like many of the kids in my community, Jess has an undying devotion for the four-legged members of his family. He wrote this piece as part of his culminating project called *My Life in ABC Order.*

D is for Dogs

Rodeo was a short haired collie. She was there from the day I was born to the day in June of 2010 when we had to put her down because of a neuro-logical disorder. But let me start at the beginning.

Some of my earliest memories are with Rodeo, like riding around on her back. She was my chauffer; I was some lucky kid who could use her at my disposal. My next memory is kind of bitter, but my fault. I was about five years old, and somehow, I got the bright idea to kick her. She bit me in the face. Like I said, well deserved. My next memory involves glass in the elbow, but that's another story.

One day a few years back, my cousin Austin was at my house, along with my grandparents from Montana. Austin, Wyatt, and I were out playing by our road. It was a rural area, not too heavily traveled. Some deranged creature was riding his motorcycle up and down the road at about 80 miles per hour. Rodeo went to walk across the road, and he nailed her at full speed. It was hit and run. My dad and grandpa went and found the guy. It was a long night.

Rodeo ended up being fine, until about two years ago. She started hav-ing some troubles walking around. My mom had her lay down, and she just slept until the next morning. The next day, she was still having troubles and my mom took her to the vet. The vet couldn't figure out what was wrong either, so they kept her overnight. They figured out she had a tumor, caused by the contusion from getting hit. We put her down the next day.

Last year, February 27th, 2011. I was at my friend Nathan's house. My parents picked me up. I thought it was kind of funny how there was a kennel in the back of the car, and a puppy starter kit. "We're just preparing," they said. Then, as we were driving up my hill, my mom pulled her coat off her lap. There sat a beautiful golden ball of fuzz. Later that night, we named her Ella.

Ella and I have become best of friends since then. We regularly have wrestling matches in the living room. She sleeps with me sometimes, and we swim in my pond together. Dogs and I have had such great experiences together in my lifetime. I hope these experiences will last and endure.

Jess' writing is just another example of what kids can produce when we allow them to take responsibility for their writing. Kids work hard when the work matters to them.

A poem by Marissa Tallman

Marissa is a careful girl who observes before she acts. Her first piece of writing for the year showed me that she had a way with words, but she was still operating on the idea that writing at school was just an assignment. It took a while for the two of us to connect, but once trust was established, I saw the true girl through her work. "Goodbye" is an example of laying it all on the line and writing from the heart. I appreciate the honesty in this poem. Marissa wasn't writing to please anyone but her subject.

Goodbye

I miss you living up the street
a home away from home
I miss your stories, we learned so much
I always think of your scorpion story
inspiration for my first tattoo
and your roadrunner for my second.

I miss your sarcasm
stupid jokes
loving voice
carefree way
and good times.

It makes me smile and laugh
when I think of Amanda's lip piercing
and how you encouraged her
as you were fading away to Alaska.

I don't have one bad memory
but your funeral, the only one I remember crying at
I never really got to say a true goodbye
I thought you were coming back
I will miss your forever
I can never forget you.

Marissa's poem is a strong reminder of what is possible when we allow kids to write from their hearts. When kids get past writing what they think we want to read or for a grade, authentic text emerges. And while a poem like this one will make up only a small amount of the writing that Marissa will do in her academic life, her more structured and formal writing will always carry a piece of her within it. She takes away the knowledge that no matter the format, she is to be present in her writing.

▌ What About Writing That Isn't Self-Directed?

You may be wondering about the more academic writing—five-paragraph essays, writing for tests, research projects. It would be neglectful not to prepare students for the kinds of writing they'll encounter during their school years. Teachers of writing need to consider this balance when determining what writing will look like in their classroom.

But if we jump right into teaching the formal essay or the research paper, we're making writing just another assignment that teachers ask students to do. If we don't allow time for kids, especially middle school kids, to make the connection between writing and themselves, what they write might never fully be a part of them; instead, they may become that next generation of adults who panic when they have to write anything.

I can tell you with certainty that the kids whose work you read went from writing about what was most important to them to writing more

> **The kids whose work you read went from writing about what was most important to them to writing more formally structured essays with minimal difficulty.**

formally structured essays with minimal difficulty. The toughest part for them is accepting that someone else is going to determine the subject of their work (as in prompts for standardized tests). They see this as totally unfair! But they understand that not all writing opportunities in life are going to be self-determined. The real world is full of responses to literature, reports for jobs, requests for information, essay questions for college applications, and project proposals.

■ Enduring Skills for Confident Writers

The advantage that Maryanne, Anthony, Adair, Jess, and Marissa have over students whose sole writing focus is formally structured test essays is that they got to know the essential processes for writing while working on pieces that mattered to them. They worked through the writing process when their subject was personal and their desire to be clear, concise, and understood was high. That confidence will endure, and it doesn't matter whether their future writing is of their choosing or something assigned by a superior.

Changes in how your students approach writing may appear sooner than you think! Of course, you'll see growth in your students over the course of a year. For proof, keep a sample of students' beginning-of-the-year writing, and read those pieces when the year is over. You'll be amazed! Also, you might begin to hear comments from other teachers, both in other disciplines and at higher grade levels, about how students are responding to writing tasks in their classes. Maybe a language arts teacher in the next grade will mention that in the past students found it almost impossible to begin an essay answer or a reflective piece, and now they get to work right away, without hesitation. Maybe another teacher will pull you aside and say, "I wanted to tell you that over the last few years, my eighth graders' writing in science has improved greatly! They are willing and skillful writers! Thanks for doing what you do!" These comments are clear indications that your students know that writing goes beyond the four walls of your classroom. What you've taught them endures!

People may question your methods. They may want to know why you aren't teaching the kinds of writing that are "useful" in life. Remember, some people have a very narrow view of what constitutes important writing. They may not realize that a well-rounded writer can communicate through many avenues and that the writing skills necessary in one genre bleed into others. Do your best to communicate the importance of writers connecting with their writing and how the confidence this engenders, coupled with the skills students are taught, results in writers who can tackle just about any task put before them. You, too, need to be confident in what you know to be true. With a logical explanation for why you do what you do and an eventual track record of happy kids, skilled writers, and high test scores, it won't take much to satisfy naysayers.

Above all, don't skip the step in which kids are allowed to make writing their own. Give them the chance to meet writing eye to eye. You can't guarantee that writing will be easy; you *can* tell them that their skills and confidence level will always allow them to face all kinds of writing challenges and find ways to create meaningful and purposeful text.

7

Where Do We Go from Here?

Becoming Even Better

ONCE WE ALLOW OURSELVES TO BE STUDENTS OF WRITING, we become more comfortable as writing teachers. Teaching writing becomes a way of life. Our work is not a job, it is a profession. We think about our lessons in the middle of the night. Reading a magazine article sparks a new writing project. We watch for new, fresh genres and formats that may interest our students. We seek out the like-minded, knowing that the thoughts and practices of others make our own stronger. Our constant desire is to make our students' writing experiences richer and more meaningful. We realize that what we do outside our hours in the classroom impacts the instruction we provide our writing students.

> **Teaching writing becomes a way of life.**

The following ideas are divided into two sections: what we can do at school to build support and community, and what we can do outside our school day to enrich our writing life and the writing lives of our students.

▌At School

In the best-case scenario, we'll be surrounded by other teachers who see the importance of how children are taught to write. We can turn to one another for support, ideas, and collaborative planning. If this describes your situation, consider yourself lucky!

In reality, you might find yourself alone as you embark on this adventure. If you talk to other teachers in your building and they initially write off your ideas as faddish or make statements like, "Oh, I tried that, and it didn't work," you may have to go it alone for a while until you find someone brave enough to join you. People in our profession are wary of new things that come along and with good reason. Think how quickly programs, demands, curriculum, and materials come and go! We are masters at trying everything but never sticking with anything long enough to make it work. Your colleagues may see your foray into writing workshop as another trip around the "what's new?" block, and, really, that's okay. Just give them time.

> **Your colleagues may see your foray into writing workshop as another trip around the "what's new?" block, and, really, that's okay. Just give them time.**

They'll begin to see a change in students' reactions to your class. They'll see a change in how kids relate to you. Continue to talk about what is happening in your room. Share your successes: "Read this piece Sally wrote about the first time she got off the ski lift at Stevens Pass!" Other teachers will start to wonder what you are doing to pull such good and real writing from kids. Trumpet the enthusiasm your students have for writing. If your school has morning announcements, arrange to have some of your students read the poems they've written. Get their work into school newsletters, on hallway walls, and in display cases. Most of all,

> **Talk about what is happening in your room. Share your successes.**

make sure others see how much you enjoy what you are doing: many folks find it hard to fathom why anyone would find such fulfillment in teaching writing in middle school.

Once others in your department see what you are doing (and perhaps notice that your students' test scores have gone up), they might be more willing to join you. It is then your job to bring them along, letting them benefit from your experiences and at the same time creating that community we all so desperately need. Arrange to meet regularly to plan and to

> Shared experiences
> create a culture of
> writing in your school.
> . . .Teaching writing is
> hard work, but if we
> love the process, love
> our students, and
> love the people with
> whom we work, it is
> that much sweeter.

work through problems. Be sounding boards for one another, sharing new ideas and venting frustrations. The conversations you have around student work, struggles, breakthroughs, successes, and challenges will bring to light the very best ways to help your students and one another. The shared experiences you have as teachers of writing will bind you together with common pedagogy and vocabulary. These shared experiences create a culture of writing in your school. Out of this culture arise opportunities to publish student work, organize extracurricular writing events, and integrate writing into other content areas. Teaching writing is hard work, but if we love the process, love our students, and love the people with whom we work, it is that much sweeter.

▉ Outside School

As we become attuned to the process of writing, a multitude of thoughts about teaching and learning and the writing process come to us outside school. Out in the world, all kinds of opportunities challenge and strengthen our skills as writers and writing teachers. Here are a few possibilities.

Listen to authors

A wonderful and rewarding gift you can give yourself as a writing teacher is to listen to authors talk about their writing. Look for universities and bookstores that bring authors of all kinds in to talk, read their work, and sign books. I've been fortunate to hear Lois Lowry, Christopher Paul Curtis, Pam Muñoz Ryan, David Guterson, Anthony Horowitz, Chris Crutcher, Laurie Halse Anderson, John Green, and many others talk, not only about their books but also about how they write. Authors are great at sharing their processes. You'll be encouraged by their tales of struggle, of the times the right words just won't show up on the paper. Sometimes they show photographs of their families (and explain family members' connections to the characters they create) and the places in which they write. You'll learn all kinds of cool things: Lois Lowry does the photography for many of her book covers; Christopher Paul Curtis started writing stories during his breaks in an automobile manufacturing plant; Anthony Horowitz bases the antagonists in his books on the teachers he had in school. Go hear the famous and the not-so-famous. Any opportunity you have to listen to others talk about their writing is worth your time.

If you are enriched by what authors tell you about their practice, your students will be too. Reinforce your message about the importance of revision by telling students that some authors spend 10 percent of their time composing and 90 percent revising. Let your students know that many authors use their childhood friends and enemies as the basis for the characters in their books. Sharing what you learn is giving away the secrets to writing success and allowing students to peek into the Authors' Club. By going to listen to authors, you show your students that you are learning, that you seek out opportunities to listen to and learn from the people who write books for a living. If you can't find live events, seek out recordings of authors talking about and reading from their work. You can play these podcasts, videos, and audio recordings for your students as well.

Find your tribe and gather

If you can't find support for teaching writing within your building, fear not. You can connect in numerous ways, both in cyberspace and in person.

Find a blog that supports your teaching; better yet, start your own. Sharing the struggles, problems, and victories of teaching writing helps you process your practice and may help others too. Virtual communities provide support and encouragement for all involved. The websites of professional teaching organizations offer articles, web chats, ideas, and message boards: all are chances to connect with people who will understand your difficulties and celebrate your successes.

> Sharing the struggles, problems, and victories of teaching writing helps you process your practice and may help others too.

You can also find support through face-to-face encounters. If you do not have the support you desire within your building, chances are you'll find like-minded people in a regional education organization for literacy teachers. If your local literacy group is weighted toward reading, encourage them to bring in more speakers on writing. Better yet, volunteer to be a speaker yourself, and show everyone how you approach writing instruction in your classroom. By sharing your story, you'll show that writing instruction (which, remember, is scary to many) can be conducted in ways that create good all-around writers.

Closer to home you might find writing groups, community education writing classes, and writing retreats. Whatever the focus of these events, all of them get participants writing and interacting with one another. In these groups you'll find all kinds of writers, from hobbyists to published professionals. The range of experience and expertise, as well as support and advice, can boost your skills and confidence—all within a social environment.

Organizations like the National Council of Teachers of English and the National Writing Project hold regional and national conventions and workshops. There, over a long weekend, you'll find more sessions on writing than you could ever hope to take in. You'll be surrounded by people who "get" you and understand the trials and tribulations of being a writing teacher. These events may require a bit of travel, but they are well worth the effort.

Read, read, read

It's no big secret that writers read. Reading gives us ideas to ponder, introduces us to new structures and genres, and helps us develop our confidence and skills as writers and writing teachers.

As a middle school teacher you've probably figured out that not many education books out there are written exclusively for us. Scanning shelves in bookstores and pages in catalogs, we find a plethora of titles aimed at elementary and high school teachers. Books about middle school instruction are fewer and thinner.

What do we do? We become experts at gleaning from books written for all levels, adapting them to the processes in our classroom. We get great ideas for classroom organization from books written for elementary teachers. Books for elementary teachers also remind us that writing cannot happen in isolation, that it is a process that affects all disciplines. Books written for high school teachers remind us of the importance of depth, that there is always more to learn. Literary journals, usually published by professional or research organizations, give us fresh ideas to consider, reminding us that the issues we encounter with student writing might be better addressed through another channel. Even the articles or books that go against every fiber of our belief about how to teach writing give us strength to continue our demanding yet rewarding path. All kinds of books on an array of subjects are out there to learn from, as long as we don't get too hung up on grade levels and are flexible enough to adapt ideas to a middle school context.

The reading we do for pleasure (you have that kind of time, right?) also benefits our writing and teaching. When you run across a passage that is interestingly or beautifully worded, mark it and use it as an example in a writing lesson. Buy and read young adult fiction so that you'll not only be able to recommend great books to your students but also have an entire library of examples to share when your students are writing. Examining the writing of a published author is an excellent way to model effective writing for students, especially if they are writing in the same genre.

Write, write, write

In earlier chapters I've talked about how your students benefit from having a writing teacher who writes. Writing, whether formally or informally, keeps you in touch with the processes your students encounter. You become an empathetic collaborator. Students see you walking your talk, especially when you share your work and the inspiration behind your pieces.

Keep a journal. Write a blog. Go on a writing retreat. Write your memoir or your autobiography. Write and publish an article on your practices so that you might help others along the way. Conduct an action research project, and write about the results. Go after that Great American Novel. Write a poem, and give it to your best friend as a birthday gift. Write a letter to your mother. Just write. No doubt your life is busy, but even fifteen minutes a day keeps you in touch with the craft. Allow writing to help you decompress. Do it for yourself, and do it for your students. You won't be sorry.

> **Go after that Great American Novel. Write a poem, and give it to your best friend as a birthday gift. Write a letter to your mother. Just write.**

▌ Here We Are at the End, Which Is Really a Beginning

We've moved through all the steps in the diagram in Chapter 1, but as with any spiral, the ending is really a beginning. Each pass through the process makes you a better teacher of writing and a better teacher in general! The growth you and your students experience compels you forward, reminding you that amazing things are possible if you keep pushing ahead.

I hope that what you've read, considered, digested, and implemented here has been useful. I hope parts of this book have inspired you to make your classroom a place in which all are valued, all are enriched, and all make incredible writing progress. You have taken on a role of great importance, guiding your students through the murky waters of early adolescence in a profession that scares even the bravest souls. The purpose of these last words is to inspire you to keep doing this important work, especially in times that feel demanding and difficult.

Remember that all children can write. All children deserve the freedom and confidence to take pen to paper to solve their problems, share their feelings, create something meaningful, and change the world.

Remember that there is no magic formula for a writing class, no curriculum that will tell you what to do when. Keep your eyes open and your ear to the ground. Watch for what your students need and for the writing that tells you your students have connected with the process. Every day, do your best to bring real writing into your classroom. Make sure your students understand that writing is messy, difficult, and terribly satisfying all at the same time. Let them see you sweat through your own writing struggles. Show them what writers do, especially when writing seems impossible, and how writers get inspired to keep making progress. Make sure your students know each and every day that you love them, respect them, and care for them, not only in your writing class but in all their endeavors.

> **In time, your students will find that they cannot hide behind their words—that they'd rather stand behind them.**

And don't forget to nurture yourself as a writer. Continue to work through your own struggle, remembering that it is what it is. Keep writing for yourself. Find others who see writing and writing instruction as you do. Grow through the observations and wisdom of others. While your writing class is all about your students, it begins with you, as a confident writing teacher, standing at the ready, with the wisdom to know that you don't know it all, that not always having the answers is part of the writing process and the process of teaching writing.

Whether or not you realize it, you are in a unique situation as a middle school writing teacher. Daily, you have the opportunity to know your students on a level that is much more difficult to achieve in other disciplines. In time, your students will find that they cannot hide behind their words—that they'd rather stand behind them. Through you, they'll discover that one cannot write authentically without being known. Your students will know you in a unique way too. They will leave your class enriched by your example, a teacher who not only taught them the power of writing but also let them into your life through your own writing and conversations. They'll leave as confident writers, not because of some state writing test score but because they've had real writing instruction, based on a solid process, and tackled meaningful topics from their own lives. As an added benefit, your students leave you knowing what it is like to be part of a community, part of a group in which they feel acknowledged, accepted, and valued. They won't forget this feeling, and many will go on to create this community for others, bringing comfort and inclusion to the people in their future lives.

Lots of people can teach, but not everyone can teach middle school. Bless you for having the wherewithal to stand before kids during the squirreliest, wildest, most irresponsible, most unpredictable, most obtuse, and sometimes most unlikable time of their lives, so that they may come to know their awesome potential as writers and as people. While you might never see the outcome of your influence, rest assured that the impact you have on your students' lives is like the rings on the surface of a pond. You are the rock dropped into the water, creating ever-widening ripples of understanding.

Quite honestly, I can't think of anything more noble and important, can you?

> **While you might never see the outcome of your influence, rest assured that the impact you have on your students' lives is like the rings on the surface of a pond. You are the rock dropped into the water, creating ever-widening ripples of understanding.**

Appendix

Roll Questions

1. Are you the oldest, youngest, middle, or only child in your family? Where do you fall in the lineup?

2. How did your parents choose your name?

3. Tell us about your pets (how many, kinds).

4. It's your birthday, and you get to choose the restaurant. Where will your family dine?

5. Are you a spender or a saver?

6. You've won a prize of two million dollars. You get to keep one million, and you must give the second million to an organization that makes the world a better place. Which organization(s) will you choose?

7. If you could paint your room any color you wanted, what color would you choose?

8. You get to invite someone to dinner. Who will it be?

9. What is your least favorite food?

10. What frightened you when you were a little kid?

11. Who makes you laugh the hardest?

12. Who is your oldest friend?

13. Show us your best scar (that is not under clothing!), and tell us how you got it.

14. When have you been lucky?

15. What have you lost that you've never found again?

16. What is your favorite spot in your house?

17. If you could change one thing about our school building, what would it be?

18. What would you like to learn to do before your life is over?

19. What is the nicest thing anyone has ever done for you?

20. If you could give a gift to anyone, what would it be?

21. What is something you do well?

22. What is something you don't do well?

23. What is your favorite sport to watch and your favorite sport to play?

24. What is your dream car?

25. If you could solve one world problem, what would it be?

26. What is your favorite thing to do in the snow?

27. Who is your favorite relative outside your immediate family?

28. If you could change your name, what would you choose?

29. You have one week, and you get to travel anywhere in the United States. Where would you go?

30. What creeps you out?

31. If your favorite dessert was sitting in front of you right now, what would we see?

32. On a scale of 1–10, how strict are your parents?

33. What birthday has been your favorite so far?

34. What age are you looking forward to and why?

35. If you could choose to have any beverage come out of the drinking fountain at school, what would you choose? (School appropriate, please!)

36. What is your favorite class at school?

37. Who has been your favorite teacher?

38. If could receive any gift, what would it be?

39. What is the best smell in the world?

40. When you are older, will you live in a big city, a town, or out in the country?

41. What is your favorite loud noise?

42. What is the most incredible weather event you've ever been through?

43. If you could write for a magazine or newspaper, which one would you choose?

44. If you won a million dollars, what would you be doing right now?

45. If you had to choose a letter for your name, what letter would you choose?

46. If you could do something daring and you were guaranteed not to get hurt, what would you do?

47. What is your favorite month of the year and why?

48. If you could have anything delivered to your house each morning, what would it be?

49. What is something you have lost or broken that you'd like to get back again?

50. When you are having a bad day, what cheers you up?

51. What is your favorite movie?

52. Let's say snow can fall in a flavor and a color. Which would you choose?

53. What is a vacation you'd like to take someday?

54. If you could fly over any city, monument, structure, or place in the world, what would you choose to fly over?

55. When do you wish you'd had a video camera so that you might be $10,000 richer?

56. If you could wake up every morning and look out a picture window at a perfect view, what would you see?

57. You get to watch one television show per week for an entire year. Which one would you choose?

58. What artifact would you like to own?

59. If you could compete in any Olympic event, what would it be?

60. If you won two million dollars tomorrow, what is the first thing you'd do or buy?

61. How would your parents describe you in one word? Your teachers? Your best friend? Your enemy?

62. What is something you really like to do that others consider boring?

63. What is something you own that has sentimental value but little or no monetary value?

64. If you could bring back one deceased person, famous or not, whom would you choose?

65. You get to swap lives with a friend for a month. Whom would you choose?

66. In your opinion, what is the Eighth Wonder of the World?

67. If you could create a new month and add it to the year, what would you call it and where would you place it?

68. Time travel has become a possibility! If you were to travel back (to George Washington's time) what modern-day device would you take along to share?

69. If you could have a Costco pallet of anything other than money, what would you want?

70. What job do you know you don't want to do as an adult?

71. What job(s) do you think you'd like to have?

72. What is the best thing about your home?

73. If you could stand at the pinnacle of any object or structure, which would you choose?

74. What is difficult for you to remember?

75. What is the longest line you've ever stood in?

76. Say temperature stays constant. What is the perfect year-round temperature for you?

77. What is one of your family's holiday traditions?

78. Who are the top five on your Very Important People list?

79. What did you learn the hard way?

80. Fill in the blank: Today would be the best day in the world if when I got home _____ .

81. What will be the best thing and the worst thing about leaving home?

82. Which moment from your life would you choose to relive?

83. What's the difference between how you see yourself and how others see you?

84. Which language would you like to learn to speak?

85. If you were to become an exchange student for a year, where would you like to live?

86. If you were stuck in the wilderness, how likely would you be to survive (scale of 1–10)?

87. What is your biggest pet peeve?

88. What do you appreciate most about your parents?

89. On Saturday, you hear your parents say, "We are going _____ shopping." What is the worst kind of shopping?

90. Would you choose to be the worst player on a winning team or the best player on a losing team?

91. What three words describe how you feel right now?

92. What is a moment in your life you'll never forget?

93. When you are away from home for a while, what do you miss most?

94. If you could rename the street you live on, what would it be?

95. What is the best thing you can cook or bake?

96. What is the best drive/road trip you've been on?

97. You win a trip anywhere in the country for four people. A parent takes up one spot; you take up the second. Who will the other two travelers be, and where will you go?

98. What is the best part of summer/fall/winter/spring?

99. You get to step into a book or story and live there. Which would you choose?

100. What is one of your artistic talents? One of your athletic talents?

Works Cited

Atwell, Nancie. 1998. *In the Middle: New Understandings About Writing, Reading, and Learning.* Portsmouth, NH: Heinemann/Boynton/Cook.

Dickinson, Emily. 1924. *The Complete Poems of Emily Dickinson.* Boston: Little, Brown.

Fletcher, Ralph, and JoAnn Portalupi. 2004. *Teaching the Qualities of Writing.* Portsmouth, NH: Heinemann/Firsthand.

Poemhunter. "Matsuo Bashō Poems." www.poemhunter.com/i/ebooks. Last accessed February 12, 2013.